ENDORSEMENTS

Dr. Young's first book, *Fight or Flight*, captured the gritty truth of the day-to-day challenges hostage negotiators endure on the job. His follow-up book, *When Every Word Counts*, dives even deeper into this line of work. He not only details the profound and dark stressors that impact everyday people and lead to these times of crisis, but he also captures the successful, daring, and sometimes remarkable response of the law enforcement community to mitigate and deescalate these dangerous situations. This book is a must-read for those interested in law enforcement, and for those charged with implementing the best practices for hostage negotiation teams across the globe.

Michael Falk, Lieutenant, New York Police Department
Commanding Officer, Hostage Negotiation Team

I had the pleasure of collaborating with Dr. Andy Young during 2019 whilst we were delivering negotiator training in the UK. Andy's knowledge and passion for the negotiator specialism are exceptional. His desire to mentor newly trained negotiators was plainly evident, be it through his coaching skills or capturing learning opportunities for the students by articulating positive outcomes, as well as the difficulties faced, at crisis negotiation incidents.

This new collection of real-life events and crises expertly portray the risks faced by law enforcement on a daily basis, and provide a first-hand account of the challenges experienced by all those involved. An engaging, thought-provoking read, it once again puts the spotlight on the selfless, courageous work done by first responders. This book is an essential read for all negotiators, the wider law enforcement family, and those with an interest in mental health and protecting the vulnerable within our communities.

Colin Harper, Inspector, Ret.
Police Scotland, Lead of the Police Scotland Hostage and
Crisis Negotiation Unit

Once again Dr. Young places the reader in the shoes of the Negotiator and what we go through on a day to day basis. It's been said time and time again, "You can't possibility know what I go through unless you wear the badge." Although that is a true statement, Dr. Young gets you as close as anyone can. He also shows us who wear the badge that we are not alone in our struggles. I have been the Team Leader for the North Texas Hostage/Crisis Negotiation Unit for over ten years, and I can relate personally to many of these stories. We often forget how much we have struggled and the hard lessons we have learned as time goes by. So, when we bring on new negotiators who were not yet born when we graduated high school, we want to help them avoid the same mistakes we made. This book will be a must read for my new team members so they will have a broader understanding of what negotiators go through. My hope is that you will enjoy this book as much as I have.

John Vance, President
Texas Association of Hostage Negotiators

In *When Every Word Counts*, Andy Young takes the reader along on a variety of typical negotiation team callouts. Media-intense high-profile prison riots, terrorist takeovers, skyjackings, and bank robbery hostage situations are, in truth, rare. Few police negotiators will ever work one of these events. While no less dangerous or stressful, police negotiators are more often called to respond locally to tense situations of high emotion, often involving desperate and/or suicidal individuals, commonly acting from anger, rage, or frustration over life events or relationships gone bad. Dr. Young does a great job sharing his personal experiences of responding to and resolving these challenging situations, demonstrating compassion and understanding to gain trust. Most are resolved peacefully using the approaches and communication skills Dr. Young describes, yet danger is always lurking and an unexpected turn of events can quickly result in tragedy for all involved. If you want to know what the life of a typical police hostage negotiator is all about, reading this book is well worth your time.

Gary W. Noesner
Chief, FBI Crisis Negotiation Unit (retired)
Author: *Stalling for Time: My Life as an FBI Hostage Negotiator*

WHEN EVERY WORD COUNTS

AN INSIDER'S VIEW OF CRISIS NEGOTIATIONS

DR. ANDREW T. YOUNG, *LPC-S, NCC*

Publisher—Stillman Publishing
Lubbock, Texas

Library of Congress Cataloging-in-Publication Data

Library of Congress Control Number: 2020906782

ISBN: 979-8-9862749-2-8 Paperback
          979-8-9862749-3-5 eBook

To all the men and women in emergency services who all too often are called upon to do an impossible job:

my deepest admiration and respect.

I am sending you out like sheep among wolves.

—Matthew 10:16

TABLE OF CONTENTS

FOREWORD

Hostage or crisis negotiators are a distinct group within law enforcement who attempt to resolve high-crisis situations with their words while displaying the ability to remain calm under emotionally demanding circumstances. Demonstrating self-control is one of their most critical attributes. The negotiator is expected to possess the capability of setting aside his or her own emotions during difficult negotiations, approaching the situation in a non-judgmental way, and, in most instances, doing so in a congruent and amenable manner. Much easier said than done! Most encounters are hostile; the other party, "the bad guy" as Andy calls them (the hostage taker or barricaded wanted criminal) becomes angry because the negotiator is interrupting his or her plans. The same could be said about someone whose life is spiraling out of control and finding himself or herself perched on the girder of a bridge, or on the tenth-floor garage landing near the Texas Tech University football stadium, convinced that suicide is the only option.

Andy then validates that the negotiator is expected to bring a lifetime of personal experience to the table in order to manage the potentially volatile and life-altering encounter to an efficacious conclusion. Negotiators, then, must be the calming voice of reason in the most unreasonable and chaotic of situations. A good negotiator must be a mature and stable individual who can adapt to quickly changing circumstances. Andy demonstrates this crucial quality in his account of many highly unpredictable encounters, helping the reader to understand that in each case the stakes are high: if the negotiator fails in the negotiation attempt, lives could very well be lost.

I first met Andy a few years back at a hostage negotiation conference in Las Vegas where we both were invited to speak. We were immediately drawn to each other by our shared work in the field of crisis negotiation: he in Lubbock, Texas and me in New York City, where I led the New York City Police Department's (NYPD) hostage negotiation team for 14 years. I recall him making fun of my New York City accent, to which I retorted, "Seriously?" after listening to his Texas twang! I noted almost immediately Andy's passion and belief in what he was doing and saw a younger version of me in him. I was also passionate about the work that I did, and still am in teaching hostage negotiations around the country as well as internationally. So, I was immediately hooked on Andy Young! Our resumés mirror each other in many ways, except of course, in the area of academics. Where Andy achieved his Doctorate in Counselor Education (he did ask me to lose the doctor title as soon as I met him), I have had great difficulty in getting through high school math. I did go on to achieve my Master's Degree in Criminal Justice before retiring from the NYPD with 34 years of service, which was a major accomplishment for me! During my career with NYPD, I served sixteen years in the Emergency Service Unit, NYPD's version of SWAT in three ranks (police officer, sergeant, and lieutenant) and during my last 14 years, I also served as the commander of the Hostage Negotiation Team.

In this book, Andy speaks of the complexities of managing life-and-death encounters with people in crisis and brings to life his extensive knowledge and operational experience that will serve as a learning document for hostage negotiators and SWAT members everywhere. I believe this work strikes the balance of illustrating a difficult job with a light-hearted touch in just the right places. It will appeal to negotiators, SWAT operators, as well as those in the non-law enforcement community. He emphasizes the importance of respecting the process of controlling the emotion of not only the subject, but also of the negotiator. He points out through numerous examples that whenever a decision is made in high emotion, more often than not, there will be an unfavorable outcome. He demonstrates through his stories that crisis negotiators must adapt to volatile hostage and related events by being extremely patient, lowering subjects' expectations, and reversing their sense of empowerment and control. Negotiators use time to allow subjects the space to vent their emotions, and to initiate give-and-take bargaining (making subjects a partner in resolving the crisis). At the same time, the tactical team (SWAT) uses highly visible containment strategies to demonstrate to the subject that the police are willing and able to use force, if absolutely necessary. Still, Andy is quick to clarify that the police should never directly threaten to use force because doing so may cause subjects to resist further, misinterpreting the threats as an ultimatum.

Andy takes the reader into the intense inner perimeter of police work where he demonstrates, in firsthand accounts, how the often thankless and unsung heroes of policing, the hostage negotiators and SWAT team, go far and beyond anything that the news media will ever be able to report, and of how their committed, tireless dedication and passion have saved countless lives.

Jack Cambria
Lieutenant, New York Police Department (Ret.)
Hostage Negotiating Team Commander
Emergency Services Unit
New York, NY

PREFACE

It took a lot to write my first book. Only a miracle enabled me to complete my doctoral dissertation in 2003, much less write a whole book. Ever since *Fight or Flight* came out in 2015, I keep getting the same question: When will you write another? For three years that question remained a splinter in my brain. I tried to remove the splinter by writing a series of stories that didn't make it into the first book, but eventually that series got so long that it became the size of another book. So, here is my effort to remove that splinter by getting it all on paper again.

I have always found it therapeutic to teach about crisis intervention and tell my stories in class. Since writing *Fight or Flight*, I've enjoyed the added pleasure of bringing my stories and lessons learned to academic and professional conferences. I love teaching, and I love speaking about these calls and about how to intervene in crises. Writing down these stories accomplishes some personal benefit for me as well, and I highly recommend it to others. Cops, medics, firefighters, counselors—we all need to process and then expel the toxins associated with crisis; otherwise, these toxins (thoughts, images, and feelings) will start to rot us out from the inside. Write, speak, and talk to your friends; get it out. As helpers, we naturally try to protect others, and often do so at our own expense. We protect others by holding in the toxins, but this inadvertently creates a distance between us and our loved ones. Our loved ones know something is going on with us, but if we remain silent, we hurt ourselves by keeping those toxins in, and we also underestimate those around us. They may be stronger than we think, and they may even benefit from hearing our stories, no matter how sad, depressing, scary, or gruesome they are. I have been blessed to be able to share my stories with people who want to hear them and learn from them. My audiences hear of our bad days, the days we "lose" the fight, the days we are not able to help someone else make the right choice, and they are supportive and tell me they take those lessons back to their departments and their teams and implement the lessons learned. I love that.

I told a story in the first book about negotiating with a man high on methamphetamines and trying to get up his courage to commit suicide-by-cop. It was a horrible experience for us all because I/we could not stop him, and so we watched him die at our feet. Since that call, we have had another callout that was eerily similar. Many of us at that first callout were now responding to this one. However, we learned things from that first callout, and now we get to tell this new story and its much happier conclusion.

The preface for this book remains the same as the one for the first book: the incidents herein described include, for the most part, a spectrum of horrific crises and sometimes criminal activity. I have omitted real names when speaking of a victim or perpetrator; however, I often use the term "bad guy" when referring to a person who, without a doubt, has committed a crime. (My cop friends use more colorful language.)

I proudly serve and assist the officers, dispatchers, and staff of the Lubbock Police Department (LPD), who always do the best they can with the information and resources they have available. I've experienced up-close and firsthand the immense pressure of their responsibilities. Thus, I can say with certainty that law enforcement officers and emergency services personnel do some of the most difficult and thankless work, non-stop, every day and every night, amidst various circumstances of chaos and crisis—many times finding themselves in dangerous predicaments where stability comes from relying on their wits, training, and the officers backing them.

The purpose of this book is to help others who may also be in this line of work. My hope is that sharing my stories, experiences, and lessons learned might also educate those who only have a vague understanding of what transpires on the other side of the yellow tape and in amongst the flashing red and blue lights. I am an educator at heart, so I trust that what I am about to share will be beneficial. These are my stories...

ACKNOWLEDGMENTS

Thank you to my wife, Stacy, who, while I am out with the police, entrusts my safety to God, takes care of the many responsibilities at home, and supports me fully even when this work personally or adversely affects me.

Thank you to all the men and women of the Lubbock Police Department (LPD) who have been notably supportive of me, and the Victim Services Crisis Team, and who have entrusted me with a great and serious responsibility.

Thank you to everyone who has served or continues to serve on the Victim Services Crisis Team at the LPD. It has been a privilege to work alongside such an outstanding group of people.

Thank you to the SWAT and Negotiating Teams at LPD. I have always considered it an amazing honor to be a part of these teams and this work. Special thanks to Assistant Chief Neal Barron, Assistant Chief Nathan White, Lieutenant Eric Quijada, Lieutenant Nathan Anderson, Sergeant Sharon Casey, and everyone on the team, past and present.

Thank you to my friends and colleagues in the field of hostage (crisis) negotiations. Among them are Dr. Wayman Mullins, Dr. Michael McMains, Lieutenant Jack Cambria, Sergeant Brandon Pierpoint, Inspector Andy Brown, Inspector Colin Harper, Special Agent London "Max" Howard, Sergeant Bill Kidd, Lieutenant Mark Lowther, Special Agent Mike Yansick, Sergeant Harry Drucker, Staff Sergeant Sean

Pollack, Staff Sergeant Gary McDougal, Chief Sam Farina, and Special Agent Tom Strentz.

Thank you to my supportive friends and family, and my co-workers at LCU. These include my parents, in-laws, Seydia Adkins, Neil Sinclair, bandmates, Becky Stroman, LaLani Carter, and Michael Hardin.

INTRODUCTION

Although I am a counselor, college professor, crisis counselor, and hostage (crisis) negotiator, I prefer to introduce myself as the latter. After more than 20 years in these jobs, I still love what I do. I now get to supervise, train others, and speak around the nation about this work. It was a shock to discover that these great jobs have gotten even better because I get to talk about them at conferences and trainings. But this work has not been easy. I outlined this in my first book, so I won't unpack that again, but rather let this additional collection of stories do the talking. I'm glad I get to share these with people, not only for my own mental health, but hopefully to help others. It's important for people to understand what goes on after the cops show up, and I want people to know what to do if they are called upon to assist someone during a crisis.

*****

I keep a plain notebook beside my bed because today I do a lot less on-scene response and a lot more coordinating. When a Lubbock police officer takes a call or confronts a situation that seems to call for the assistance of a mental health professional, the officer will call the Victim Services Crisis Team, which is a part of the patrol division at LPD. The officer requesting us does so by radioing our dispatchers, who in turn will call me. These calls come at all hours, every day of the week. As I write this, we have just come through a holiday season. My little notebook contains entry after entry from the last decade or so. Each entry has the name of the dispatcher who called me, the address where the LPD officers were, and a quick description of why the Victims Services Crisis Team was being called out. This notebook is a testament—even a monument—to innumerable crises, traumas, heartbreaking stories, stories of grace, healing, and triumphs in the midst of darkness. The entries include one that came in at 1:00 am this past Christmas morning. Suicide.

Dispatch called as they usually do when something like this happens. We all know the depression that can sometimes accompany the holiday season. I went to bed early Christmas Eve, partly because I knew there was a good chance I would not sleep through the night. Going into the bathroom, so as not to wake my wife (not that anyone can wake my wife), I flipped on a dim light and had my notebook and pen with me. The dispatcher informed me that the man had committed suicide in front of his family, and that the family had known for a while he was going to do it, but didn't know when. I then did as I usually do: I texted the team to see who was willing and able to respond to this call for service. Two Crisis Team members answered, received the information about this call, got dressed for the weather, and headed to the address provided. And they did what they always do. They provided emotional support, a calm and empathetic listening ear, information when it was available and helpful, and follow-up calls as appropriate. Then they returned home, tried to get some sleep, and readied themselves for Christmas morning with their families, all while remembering the family from last night and what they might be going through...

There are times when I drive through Lubbock and remember a SWAT callout in that neighborhood, a traffic fatality here, the time we helped a suicidal person down from that overpass there...and it is so helpful to have in mind the many times the Crisis Team, or our SWAT negotiators, were able to bring some help, some peace, some order, some care to people in need. It is an honor and a privilege to walk this hallowed ground with these people.

*****

When I started with LPD in 2000, I did my first ride-along with a police officer, Corporal Neal Barron. Later that year, when I started working with the hostage negotiating team at LPD, one of the officers on the team was Corporal Jon Caspell. Jon would later promote to Sergeant and become the LPD supervisor for the Crisis Team. Neal would later become commander of the SWAT team. Now, almost 20 years later, it feels like Neal, Jon and I all grew up together. We have seen and been through a lot. I am now supervising the Crisis Team and speaking out of town a lot. Neal and Jon are now Assistant Chiefs who oversee entire divisions. Our most recent commander, Nathan, also promoted off our negotiating team and is an Assistant Chief. However, when there is a SWAT callout, we all show up. Their roles are a little different now, but we all work together to find the solution to the danger at hand. I love how things work out over time, and I still love this job. I especially love being a part of the hostage (crisis) negotiating team, so I believe I will begin there, especially since they gave me a bullet-resistant vest and an awesome helmet.

CHAPTER ONE

POLICE RESPONSE TO THE SUICIDAL

During those days people will seek death but will not find it; they will long to die, but death will elude them.
—Revelation 9:6

Recently I was invited to sit on a panel for a local seminar on suicide intervention and prevention. Those of us on the panel took our place on stage and were being introduced by the moderator. With bright lights in my face and a large audience in front of us my phone began to vibrate incessantly, which is usually the sign of a SWAT callout. I struggled in the moment with the social pressures that would normally keep one from checking one's phone in such a situation, but as my phone continued to vibrate I knew I needed to check it. Sure enough, I had a text message notification: "Negotiator Only Callout: Jumper, 10th floor parking garage across from the TTU football stadium, approach from the east and 10-17 with the on-scene supervisor."

Yep, I'm not making this stuff up. Who gets called out to respond to someone contemplating suicide while being on a suicide intervention panel? I now faced a tough decision. Do I leave the panel and respond to this callout? Do I just stand up and run out of the room like some socially awkward college professor (which I am)? I felt the pull of this person in need, and of the team of crisis negotiators responding to help. I made the socially bold move of getting out of my chair on stage, walking calmly over to the moderator standing at the podium, and interrupting her. I let her know what was going on, and asked her if it would be okay if I bowed out of the panel to go assist with this suicidal person. She was, of course, very understanding and gracious, and let the crowd know why I was leaving. I made my way to the scene, met our negotiator commander (Nathan), and he drove us both to the top of the parking garage. As he drove, I texted the Victim Services Crisis Team and asked if anyone could respond to this parking garage to meet with some family members who were also on scene. I then asked Nathan if I could join the two negotiators talking to this man, and he agreed.

This still image was taken from the primary negotiator's body camera.

I walked slowly over to where two negotiators were already talking to this man in distress (the photo above shows you what we saw). I did not want my approach to introduce more fear or tension into the situation, so I was mindful of walking slowly and watching for signs that my presence would make things worse. Behind the primary negotiator, who had been talking to this man for about ten minutes prior to my arrival, and behind the secondary negotiator who was coaching the primary, I took my place third in line. I put my hand on the secondary negotiator's shoulder to let him know I was there. Three things grabbed my attention in quick succession and would not let go. The first was the sight of this man's heels so far over the edge. His legs were shaking as he grabbed his head and looked around like he was completely devastated or even hallucinating. The second was the voice of the primary negotiator. Usually a baritone, in this instance, he was approaching an emphatic soprano. The third was the loud country music blaring from this individual's pickup truck. A number of other things flashed through my mind and needed triaging:

1. I hope our primary negotiator is okay because he sounds emphatic/tense.

2. We have got to get this music turned off so we can lower the inherent tension of this situation and have a more reliable channel of communication.

3. This guy is going to fall.

4. This guy has got to look at us.

5. What is going on with this guy; what is going on in his mind? Is he psychotic? Drunk? High? Emotionally overwhelmed?

6. What approach do we need to take with him and what is the key to getting through to him?

7. He has got to look at us . . .

Since my mind kept coming back to number four and number seven, I started writing it down on a three by five notecard I had with me. As I was writing, the primary negotiator was now addressing number two on my list. It is amazing to me how our team ends up reading each other's minds and is on the same sheet of music together without saying a word to each other. Sometimes we even laugh about it, as one person writes on a note card the same thing another person is thinking, and just as the primary negotiator introduces the same idea into a conversation. This manner of working together as a team is born of experience, attentiveness to other team members, training, and focus on the matter at hand.

Our primary negotiator kept talking, and when he saw my notecard he tried to get our subject to look him. He talked about our subject's kids, and suggested that our subject come down and shake hands with him. He emphasized that coming down was the right thing to do. He talked to our subject about how it would feel for our subject to move away from the edge and to come down; that coming down would be a relief, and would be the next step towards another day. Our primary negotiator just needed to keep taking and emphasizing the plan to come down. Our goal was to distract this man from any thoughts he might have of going over the edge, especially if those thoughts were not grounded in reality, but rather influenced by psychosis. We then got our subject's permission to go around to the driver's side of the pickup and turn off the music.

There were a number of times I thought we were going to lose our subject, and I could see that our primary negotiator was thinking the same thing. He came close to clapping his hands in order to get our subject's attention and hopefully startle him away from his thoughts of jumping. When our subject wasn't looking at us, or when he was looking over the edge and even turned away to look out over the city, I thought again that we were going to lose him. I prayed silently.

When our rope system and harnesses arrived, one of our negotiators came over to me to discuss the pros and cons of putting a harness on our primary negotiator, and to consider all the activity associated with getting the ropes in place. Because everything felt so precarious, we agreed it was better to wait to put on harnesses. Shortly after this, it seemed our subject was thinking about coming down and had taken a step away from the edge. We didn't want to mess up our progress, nor destroy the rapport that had developed between our subject and our negotiator. At this point, one of the patrol officers nearby, who is a longtime friend, motioned to me and made faces that asked me if he should attempt to grab our subject. I shook my head no, so he waited. The rookie officer with my friend also looked like he was going to move in, and also got waved off. It is so very difficult in situations like these to be patient and not do anything. Everyone who cares feels the pressure to do something, yet we have learned through experience that moving slowly and patiently in these types of situations usually wins the day.

Our primary negotiator had now been talking constantly for about an hour. The secondary negotiator and I kept feeding him notecards when appropriate, and it was such a relief when our subject asked about talking to his family when he came down. This, of course, was agreed to and soon our primary negotiator reviewed the come down plan: step down carefully from the ledge, walk across the front of the truck, and he and our negotiator will shake hands.

Our subject soon made his way down, and our primary negotiator said again, "Come shake my hand." You could hear and feel the sincerity and care in his voice as he said this. Our negotiator then slowly made his way around to the front of the pickup truck. As our subject got down off the ledge and a huge wave of relief washed over us all, our secondary negotiator, the negotiator right in front of me, took a step forward. Typically, the most dangerous phases of any callout are the beginning and the end, and here, again, was that pressure to do something to keep this man from changing his mind and getting back up onto the ledge. From where I stood, and based on my feel for the situation, I believed our secondary negotiator was making his move too soon, so I put my hand on the collar of his ballistic vest and held it. I did not want to spook our subject, nor ruin the good vibe our primary negotiator had going. It's similar to the feeling I had right after putting a crying baby to sleep; no sudden movements or sounds, hold your mouth just right, and never exhale.

Our subject moved around the front of the truck and shook the hand of our primary negotiator. This was both touching and a relief to behold. Now it was the right time for the negotiator in front of me to move to the front of the pickup and stand between this man and the ledge from which he had just come down. We all walked with this man down a level of this parking garage and sat down. I chatted with him a little too, but he was pretty quiet. Our primary negotiator did a great job.

We were all scared, but remained calm. And we all wondered what it was that may have helped this man make the right decision. I later reached out to the local in-patient psychiatric care facility to see if the primary negotiator and I could meet with our subject. The staff there relayed our offer, and he agreed, so we made an appointment to see him about 48 hours after he had come down from that ledge. We met him in a conference room at the facility, just the three of us. We asked him how he was doing, and he certainly looked like a different person. He seemed much more together and emotionally lighter. Our primary negotiator asked him what was helpful about our response to his situation, and he said it was good that the responding patrol officers did not crowd him. We asked what we could have done better and he asked why our primary negotiator wouldn't stop talking. I chuckled, and we explained that we had no idea what was going on with him, and we were very concerned about what seemed to be his dire train of thought in that moment. We worried that, if we didn't stop trying to communicate with him and get him to look at us, he would follow through on his thinking and we would watch him fall to his death. He seemed to understand, though he also stated he wanted some time to just catch his breath and think. He also told us that he didn't remember much from that day, that he had not slept in two days, and had not eaten or had anything to drink for about 24 hours. He was overwhelmed by relationship problems and desperate. Later in the conversation I further explained, in answer to his original question, that we were terrified that he might fall, due to his heels being so far over the edge of that ledge. He looked puzzled by what I was saying. I emphasized to him that he "scared the hell out of us" because his heels were over the edge. His face then went pale. He had no idea that he was in such a position. I almost felt bad for dousing him with this reality.

We chatted further and the tenor of the conversation was upbeat. It seemed things were headed the right way for this man, and we were glad to learn his family was also there to visit with him. We wrapped things up, shook hands, and walked out together. We met his family in the hall and they were sweet and thankful. It was encouraging to us to see such good signs regarding this man's future, and it was interesting and unexpected to learn that this man did not remember much from that day, nor knew how precarious his position was on that ledge.

I wish I could explain well enough, and have people experience what it is like to put our heart and soul into such a difficult, unpredictable, and dangerous situation. I wish they could feel how much is required of a hostage (crisis) negotiator during such an emotionally and physically draining experience. I imagine it is similar to running a marathon, but I wouldn't know because you would have to shoot at me to get me to run. It helps that we work as a team, so it is the rare occasion that one has to go through such a taxing experience alone.

It was helpful to get to sit down with this man and learn more about what was going on with him that brought him to such an emotional and desperate place. There have been times when things ended poorly and we were left with questions we could not answer. The best we could do in those times was to learn all we could based on the information we had, and try our best the next time. In my first book, *Fight or Flight: Negotiating Crisis on the Frontline*, I recounted in chapter eleven my time with Mike. He raised his machete and ran at the police officers whom I was assisting that day, and he was killed. Though we were left with a lot of questions, and the pain associated with such an incident, we also learned things that we applied to a very similar callout about a year later.

*****

Nathan (our negotiator commander) and two of our three supervisors were out of town, and I made a comment in our negotiator group text that this would be a perfect time for a callout. Shortly thereafter, a callout notification came to my phone: Armed suicidal subject and the address. We all responded, and once on scene learned that we had a man armed with a large knife and holed up in the closet of the apartment belonging to his ex-wife. Many of us who were on that previous callout with Mike were struck by the eerie similarities. We did not want this call to end in the same way. One of the first responding officers was the SWAT officer who tried to stop Mike's run at officers, with his machete raised high. He tried to stop Mike by shooting beanbags at him. On today's callout, he did not want a repeat of that horrible experience and decided to fill the hall of this current apartment with couches and pillows so our subject could not run at officers with his knife. Responding negotiators and SWAT officers positioned themselves outside of the bedroom he was in, and initiated contact from the outside of the bedroom window. These strategies came to mind because of what we had been through with Mike a year prior.

This is a photo from that day, after we all were in place and the situation had calmed a bit. It is hard to make out, but our primary negotiator has his head inside the window so he can hear. The taller officer beside him is a SWAT officer with a tool that launches multiple bean bags. That's me, on the left, doing what I can to support the primary and secondary negotiators in front of me, while also coordinating with other elements of our negotiator team (e.g. the negotiator who was sitting with the ex-wife and asking her not to respond to our subject's texts and calls, our negotiating team commander, Eric, who was with the other command staff and SWAT commander, and other members of our team who were trying to learn more about this man and the best way to help him).

This callout, which started in ways so similar to the callout I recounted in my first book, was now so very different. Now we were in front of the pitch instead of trying to catch up. We could coordinate, work as a team, and slow down this situation. I was glad about this for our primary negotiator's sake too, because this was David's first negotiation. I got to help teach his negotiator qualification course, and even played the recording of my negotiation with Mike. As I listened to David talk with this distraught man, I heard some very familiar lines, said with the same tone, empathy, meter, and intensity that I had used a year ago with Mike, "We want to take you to an ambulance…" (see page 170 of *Fight or Flight*).

For a moment, I wanted to kick David in the shin for stealing my lines, but really, I was very glad to see something good come from that horrible situation with Mike. Later in the negotiation David said, "I'm sure your ex-wife still cares about you and doesn't want you hurt." This gave me an idea. I asked the negotiator who was sitting with our subject's ex-wife to find out if she would send our subject a text along these same lines. She did, and then our subject questioned the validity of her statement. He requested to speak with her. We discussed this as a team, and also with the ex-wife (via the negotiator who was with her). She was agreeable and wanted to help. We prepared her for the phone call, and for the likelihood of our ending the call if it became unproductive. The call went okay for about 30 seconds, then not as well for about 20 seconds more, so we hung up the phone. Even with this, we were able to give our subject what he requested, and reinforced the message David was trying to relay: that he mattered to the people he cared about.

During this time, we had another dynamic to navigate: our newly-appointed chief of police. No one really knew his philosophy for handling a call like this, nor did we know how much input he would want from us when it came time for decision-making. Earlier in this callout I had made a quick comment to him, something along the lines of, "I think we are going to be here a while, Chief; I hope you're okay with that." He indicated he was, and his patience was helpful. I heard after this callout was over that Eric, for whom this was his first callout as negotiator commander, had been tested a little. Our new chief and some of the other command staff were brainstorming ideas, some of which may have been a little unorthodox, compared with the negotiator's standard of handling something like this. There started to be a consensus around the chief's ideas, and so Eric was faced with a dilemma: speak his mind to the chief and risk unexpected reprisals, or go along to get along. When he was then asked what he thought, he was clear: "I think that's a bad idea, Chief." I imagine there was a pause and that everyone was interested to see how the new chief responded to this respectful disagreement. The chief asked Eric to make his case, which he did. The chief could see where he was coming from, so we were given more time to do what we do.

It requires a lot of trust for someone in leadership to depend on and go with the recommendations of those under them. Likewise, it requires a lot of trust for those in an organization to stick their neck out and offer a different, or even opposing viewpoint on a matter. But it is this level of trust and cooperation that are the antidote for groupthink. The qualities of humility and openness also help the process of group decision-making, and all of the above are characteristics of a high-functioning organization (more on this topic in chapter three).

Soon after this, our subject was ready to come out. David reviewed the best and safest way for him to come out, and he did. He was taken to the back of a police car and all was well. Once again, we wanted to chat with this man before he was taken to the hospital, so David and I walked over to the police car and opened the door. David thanked him for working with us, and for not harming himself or others. They chatted a little and then one of us asked, "So, what was it that helped you do the right thing today?" He quickly replied, pointing at David, "Because I trust you." His words reverberated through me. This is what we want. To be trustworthy, caring, and understanding, for this to be helpful to people in crisis, and hopefully assist their decision-making. It was a good day for us all, and I was very glad that I got another try at a callout so similar to the one with Mike that had gone so poorly a year earlier.

*****

David and I worked together on another interesting callout about a year later, and one that fits with the theme of this chapter: people contemplating suicide. It is such a difficult phenomenon to understand, much less to try and intervene. Each instance is different, even when the precipitating factors are similar. The motivations for each, unique. It is a good thing we are all trained to focus on the individual, while also trying to draw from our personal and professional experiences in an effort to bring the best we can to the person before us.

On this evening, a bad guy went over to the home of his ex and her new family. There were the disagreements and differences you would expect with such an encounter, and these culminated in a 911 call. Responding patrol officers arrived to find the man in his car, engine running, with a large hunting-style knife to his neck. Officers pulled one unit close up behind this man's car, and then stood outside of his driver's side window trying to get him to come out and not hurt himself. Negotiators and SWAT were called to the scene, and David and I were the second and third negotiators to arrive.

We got a quick briefing on the situation from Eric, and then quickly determined that the patrol officers talking with this man could use our assistance. David and I walked over to the car, and then David introduced himself. I served as his coach and go-between with the command staff that was arriving. Another negotiator (Zach) arrived to assist David, which freed me to dedicate myself to passing along information about the ongoing conversation, coordinate with other elements of our response, give David and Zach information, and consult with the commanders, especially about the potential for harm to self or others.

It became clear pretty quickly that this man was not interested in talking to us, and was very focused on his ex. She even answered one of his phone calls, so once again we had a couple of negotiators sit with the ex and try to support her. Things seemed to escalate, so our team asked her not to talk to him, and she agreed. Now our subject had even fewer options. The SWAT team was arriving and getting in place, and the SWAT commander asked how much it would escalate the situation if SWAT pulled a van up in front of our subject so he could not drive off. I asked for a few more minutes to see if we were going to get anywhere via conversation with this man, and so they waited. It was soon apparent that this man would not talk to us. We were also worried he would harm himself, so I went back to the SWAT commander and outlined what I saw: This man had a knife up against his driver's side window, with the blade against his neck. He was non-responsive to us and was now unable to talk with his ex. We thought the potential for danger and/or him trying to drive off was high, and did not see that we had much choice but to try and contain his vehicle. I suggested to the SWAT commander that intervention would be needed soon and that if he saw me waving my hand, this indicated our subject was cutting himself with his knife. The commander put a plan in place for what negotiators and the SWAT operators would do if this occurred. I went back to the negotiators trying to talk to our subject, and watched as David tried to get his attention. He was unsuccessful.

The SWAT team soon drove a van up in front of this man's car and parked it, and this elicited no response from our subject. After a few more minutes we could clearly see him sawing on his neck, so I waved at the SWAT commander. David, Zach, and I backed away and the SWAT operators moved in to quickly intervene. Our subject was immediately taken to the hospital and survived.

SWAT callouts are typically very dynamic operations in the midst of very complicated and unpredictable circumstances involving people we usually know very little about. We are tasked with handling these operations with care, professionalism, speed, patience, empathy, and even violence. These callouts can last hours, and even days in some cases, and the risk to law enforcement personnel can also be very high. I hope people will have grace and understanding for us because the cards we are dealt are usually very bad and require so much of us. Here is one more difficult story to help illustrate my point.

*****

I was in bed when this call began. For whatever reason, I stirred, barely awake enough to hear a text notification when it dinged on my phone. I decided to look and it was a text from one of the negotiators on our team. Tye was on patrol and let the team know he responded to someone wanting to jump off of a very high overpass. I got dressed quickly and headed that way. When I got to my car, he texted me and asked what to do because all his subject would say was, "F you! Do not talk to me or you are going to make me jump." Tye asked what I thought he should do, and I encouraged him to be patient and not talk. I would be there in about ten minutes and try to help figure out how to talk to his angry and naked stranger.

We knew nothing about this gentleman for about three hours after meeting him. Let's call him Colter for this accounting of our seven-hour callout with him. Here's a photo of how this situation looked when I arrived. I'm the tall, skinny guy on the right. Tye, on my left, was the first negotiator on the scene. The officer in the distance is a patrol officer. He was there so Colter would not run off down the overpass, and to help if things became violent. Just because Colter was naked does not mean he wasn't dangerous. Research on police response to "naked subjects" indicates quite the opposite, and officers are oftentimes injured or killed in these situations because they are so unpredictable, and the individuals involved can be especially strong, resilient, and unpredictable.

Once again, I slowly walked up and stood next to Tye. We stood there quietly in the midnight silence and observed this man, sitting naked and hunched over in the twenty-degree weather. It was so very still and quiet, aside from the occasional car passing below us on the freeway. Tye and I were alone to handle this, for the time being, and we had nothing to go on. We did not know this man's name, and he was very clear about his demands. Every so often Tye would ask him how he was doing, asked him if he wanted anything, asked him if we could get him a blanket...all of which were met with the same response, a variant of, "F you! Do not talk to me or you are going to make me jump."

Other negotiators arrived and walked up next to, and behind us. A new negotiator, Olivia, who recently had completed her negotiator certification course, now stood to my right. Billy, a more experienced negotiator, stood behind me and we conferred. It seemed to me it was worth trying a female voice, and one that sounded as caring and as empathetic as possible. The group agreed, and we made sure Olivia was ready for her first intervention. She had a great opening line and delivered it very well. Instead of the response we'd grown accustomed to, we got silence. This caused us to become hopeful, since no response was better than, "F you." At least he was not holding us at bay and keeping us silent by threatening to jump if we talked to him.

Over the next three hours we tried several times to walk closer to him, but each time he erupted with anger and threats, so we backed away. His standard answer of, "F you! Go away! Don't talk to me or you will make me jump," eventually reemerged and was inflicted upon Olivia. It's a good thing Olivia has quite the thick skin. While this went on, other negotiators on the team were trying to track down information on our subject, and periodically found something promising. I would go back and forth between our group of negotiators and our negotiator supervisor, Sharon, to get updates and ideas. They would pass along a first name, Olivia would ask if this was his name, and we would get either no response or his standard angry response.

At some point an officer noticed a car parked about a mile away and did some checking. This led to information about a man who had a history of a psychotic disorder, drug use, and multiple arrests. We tried using this name. "Is your name Colter?" asked Olivia with a caring and helpful tone. This time Colter turned his head and peered at us through his long, dark, matted hair. "How do you spell it?" he asked. She spelled it correctly without missing a beat, and Colter went back to his original, doubled-over position. Olivia talked to him some more, offering warmth, comfort, and a listening ear, but to no avail.

Over those first few hours it became clear that Colter was affected by a psychotic disorder, and/or drug use, and this meant his body may not respond to the elements like one would expect. I thought the concrete barrier under his thighs would cut off circulation to his legs, but he was able to sit there much longer than one would have thought possible. He would periodically lift himself up, which made us nervous at first, but later it became clear he was allowing the blood flow to return to his legs and feet. Eventually he could no longer sustain this, and he climbed down from his perch and shook out his legs. It was tempting to rush Colter, but the distance was too great, and we were pretty sure he was quick enough to jump over the edge, run from us, or fight with us. So, we remained where we were, emphasizing we were trustworthy and only wanted the best for him.

We tried again to walk a little closer to him, but were met again with anger and boastful threats of harming himself and it being our fault. The way he said this though, seemed different to me: "You will make me jump." This, coupled with my experience with those who are less-than-nice people, made me wonder if he was simply trying to blame and manipulate us. I then wondered if we might be able to get away with taking some small steps towards Colter, then hold our spot when he yelled at us and threatened. We would reassure him that we were not going to rush him or grab him, that we did not want to anger him, but this time we would not be manipulated by his threats and, as peacefully and in as non-threatening way as possible, hold our ground. We decided as a group to give it a try, and it went as planned. We took a few steps forward, Colter strafed us with F bombs, and Olivia reassured him. We didn't move backwards this time, and eventually Colter went quiet again. Over the next hour, we got closer and closer to Colter, and were probably within about ten feet of him now.

Olivia turned to me during one of the many, extended pauses in our dialogue with Colter, and asked me how I thought this was going to go. I answered frankly, but also in a way to try and keep a little humor at hand. I said, "We are going to be here forever," and winked. Olivia nodded knowingly and took a deep breath. She then asked me if I thought he was going to jump. I told her there was a great chance he would, and that if he did, I was going to grab her by the belt and put my hand on her shoulder. I told her I would hold her there, and I encouraged her not to look over the edge if this happened. She agreed, and was thankful for the preparation.

During this time period, the rest of our team called the jail to see if anyone there knew Colter well, and if they had any helpful information we could use in persuading Colter to come down and get warm. We could see that his feet were turning black from the cold, and worried that they would need to be amputated. Olivia mentioned this concern to him a number of times, and pointed him to the ambulance we had standing by, just down the bridge from where we were. This all still had no effect. We also conferred as a group to decide at what point we might attempt to grab him. We agreed he needed to be in the middle of the overpass and very close to us, and that anything less would be too dangerous for him, and even for us.

I knew the program director at the jail who answered our call for information. She offered, among other things, that Colter liked burgers and might be very hungry. We conferred as a team and agreed that having some friendly faces who knew Colter, but who were also professionals who would collaborate easily with us, might be helpful on-scene. We invited the program director, and another person who worked at the jail who knew Colter well, to join us on the bridge. They brought with them a very warm looking quilt, some burgers, and hot chocolate for Colter (none for us though). I turned to Olivia and said, "Now, if they end up saying all the same stuff you've been saying for the last few hours, then you'll know you've done an outstanding job." The jail staff gave it their best shot, and indeed said everything we'd been saying. I almost high-fived Olivia right then and there.

We laid out an EMS blanket on the roadway, placed the burger and hot chocolate on the blanket, and backed away. The worker from the jail who knew Colter best held out the warm quilt and asked him to come to us. Colter walked over to the picnic area we'd assembled and put the EMS blanket around his shoulders. He drank the hot chocolate as we watched quietly from about ten feet away and resisted the urge to rush in and grab him. He then walked over to the rail again, but his legs would not work well enough for him to get back up on his perch. The workers from the jail, and then Olivia, continued their mostly one-way dialogue with Colter to no avail.

Around hour six we brought up a police car, our rope system, and a harness. We discussed rotating out the first group of negotiators because we were cold and fatigued. We then traded out most of our negotiators. Kimberlee took over for Olivia, and I stayed on so our transition might go as smoothly as possible. Colter, however, showed no signs of fatigue. His high may have been wearing off, but his psychiatric condition was not. Colter did not like seeing the negotiator with a harness, tethered to a police car. He could see he had a new issue to deal with if he wanted to continue to hold us at bay. It seemed to most of us that Colter's primary motivation was anger and pride, so we needed to provide him a way to save face if he was going to come down peacefully. Kimberlee, and then Anthony, who was in the harness, continued to reiterate the come-down plan, emphasizing the warm blanket and warm ambulance.

Around hour seven, as the freeway filled with morning commuters, Colter relented and ran to the ambulance, even with his feet looking as horrible as one might see in an Antarctic expedition documentary from the 1800's. I was amazed that, after all of this, Colter still had the energy to run to the ambulance and did not seem phased by the cold, pain, or seven hours on this overpass. He was as energetic and aware as he was at the beginning, whereas the rest of us were cold, tired, and a bit spent. Colter went to the hospital, then to the in-patient psych ward, where he proceeded to assault the staff there and be arrested. Because of this assault, he returned once again to our jail system, as do so many in our society who are suffering from a mental health condition.

Below is a view from the street level. It's hard to make out, but Colter has his feet on a little pipe that ran around the outside of the overpass. He is about 75 feet above the ground and has his chest lying over his knees, a position he maintained for much of our seven hours together.

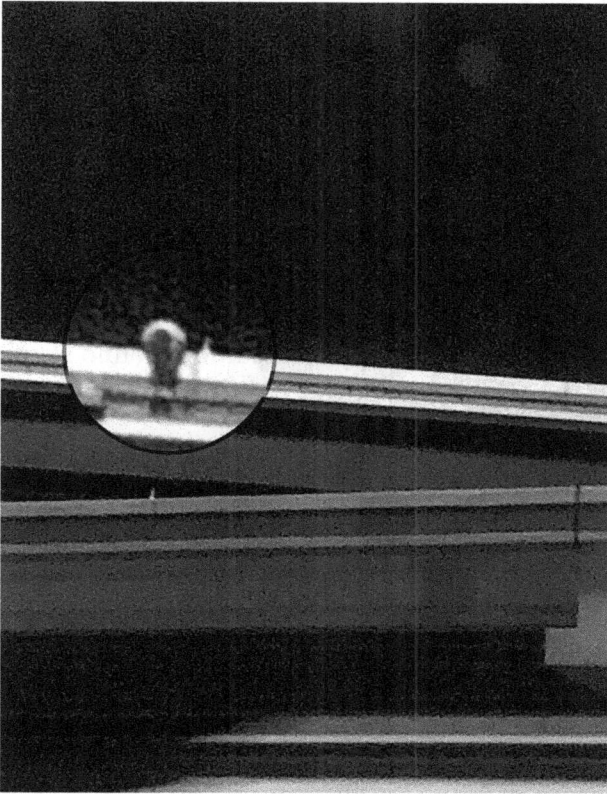

Our response to this situation represented the ultimate in patience among a caring group of professionals from law enforcement, the jail system, and mental health. I believe our patience once again ruled the day and prevented an impossible situation from becoming a tragic one. We resisted the "action imperative" (that urgent feeling that we have to do something), and slowly demonstrated our trustworthiness to this impaired, angry, and blaming stranger.

*****

Sometime after this callout I posted online the first photo from our response to Colter. My purpose in doing so was to let people know what we had been through, and to let anyone who is in a dark place know that there is support out there. I was touched and amazed to receive the following, unedited response from a woman in the Middle East:

> Hi Andy, we don't know each other. Some years ago I read Mr. Noesner's book and try to follow and read more on negotiation as it can be useful in my line of job. And I'm also writing to thank you for your compassion and great work you do out there. When I was a teenager, people talked to me on a bridge... I'm almost 41 now and despite difficulties, I found my way, and love my life. Thank you and truly all the very best.

CHAPTER TWO

THE KILL LINE

⁹The heart is deceitful above all things and beyond cure. Who can understand it? ¹⁰"I the LORD search the heart and examine the mind, to reward each person according to their conduct, according to what their deeds deserve."—Jeremiah 17:9-10

It is the rare occasion in which someone wanting to jump to their death from an elevated position poses a deadly threat to those responding to help. Those in law enforcement oftentimes enter the profession in order to help people, and it is tempting to sacrifice one's safety in order to grab someone threatening to jump, even though this is an inherently dangerous move for everyone involved. Officers certainly do not desire to kill people, but what do you do when words are not enough, or the threat is deadly? When forced to kill (e.g. in war, when trying to stop a threat or save someone else, etc.), the situation that forces one to kill and one's humanity are at odds with each other. This conflict between one's inherent humanity and the necessity to kill is frequently the genesis for Posttraumatic Stress Disorder. The intersection of humanity and a situation that requires the use of force is a complex and often difficult one. I have watched videos of a number of officer-involved shootings and seen the cognitive dissonance and gut-wrenching emotion that come forth when one is faced with having to kill. An officer's humanity often spills forth, unfiltered, and can be seen in the numerous times an officer pleads with someone whom he or she has just shot, "Why did you make me do that! Stay with me!"

Sgt. Brandon Pierpoint and I provided a training for officers in our area after reading an article by Derek Gaunt (see https://blog.black-swanltd.com/the-edge/establish-your-kill-line for details) written for *The Negotiation Edge* in 2016. The goals of this training were to see how much officers would sacrifice their safety in their effort to stop an armed suicidal subject from killing himself, and to help officers think through how to respond to a very dangerous situation while also managing their humanity and desire not to kill. Throughout this scenario-based training we could see the humanity of the participating officers on display.

Just as in Derek Gaunt's scenario, officers in our training began 45 feet away from a role player who was possibly armed with a pistol and was reported to police as being a suicidal veteran. Over 100 officers went through our scenario, and each scenario often came to a close with something like what you see below…

Responding officers and our role player often closed the distance and would be within feet of each other. The general rule in law enforcement is that a person with a knife can run at an officer and stab them if that person gets within 31 feet. Here, in our training, we were consistently seeing officers allowing someone with a gun to get within six feet. Is this a safe situation for this officer pictured above? How quickly could this suicidal veteran turn his weapon on the officer, and how much time would the officer have to perceive what was happening, aim his pistol correctly, and stop this veteran from killing the officer before killing himself? I believe it is safe to say that this officer has now sacrificed his safety and possibly his life in the hope of persuading this suicidal veteran not to hurt himself. This was the typical reaction of the majority of the officers who participated in our training.

In chapter one, I reviewed a number of different callouts we had involving suicidal subjects, and each of their motivations were different. How can an officer in a situation like the one pictured above know the motivation and lethality of a stranger? How quickly can a situation that is motivated by the desire to die turn into a situation motivated by the desire to kill? The scenario training Sgt. Pierpoint and I concocted caused officers to have to face their inner humanity that could restrain them from using lethal force, thus causing them to sacrifice their officer safety.

We tried this scenario training the first time at a monthly hostage negotiator training for the team I work with at the Lubbock Police Department (LPD). Then we tried it with the team I work with at the Lubbock County Sheriff's office (LSO), then with a varied group of deputies from the LSO, and finally for a large group of LPD patrol officers after they completed an eight-hour de-escalation training. This final group of patrol officers was the largest in our sample, and our training occurred over the course of months. Our prediction was that when officers were in a de-escalation or negotiation mindset, their officer safety mindset would be relegated to second place, and their humanity (not wanting to take a life) and desire to help someone would take first place. We also knew from experience and from Derek Gaunt's article how very difficult it would be for the officer to keep his or her weapon accurately trained on an armed subject while at the same time trying to de-escalate/negotiate with this armed, suicidal person.

Time and time again, Sgt. Pierpoint and I witnessed officers allowing this armed stranger, who they knew was a veteran (and thus probably had some proficiency with a firearm), slowly walk closer and closer to them, even when the officer issued the command to stop. Time and time again our role player would disobey the officer's commands to drop the gun. Officers most often walked backwards, many times in a circle, putting themselves in greater danger. Most of these officers who walked backwards did so for 100 feet or more, until we simply ended the scenario. How dangerous would this tactic be in the real world in which an officer has no idea what is behind him or her and could easily fall?

What was most amazing to us as we observed this scenario play out over 100 times was how often an officer's humanity burst forth, unfiltered. One example was when our role player, who was in a depressed state, holding a gun to his head and asking for help, then asked the responding officer, "Why are you pointing your gun at me?" Without hesitation, and with all the frightened emotion you would expect were this the real thing, the officer immediately shouted, "Because I'm scared!!"

I once attended a conference presentation on police officer use of expletives when trying to intervene in a situation. The researcher found that there was a strong correlation between how frightened an officer seemed to be, or reported, and their use of expletives. Most people, and I was one of them, would not think that an officer would be frightened in a situation like the one we presented in our scenario-based training. Most people don't believe an officer's angry outburst of curse words indicates fear. In hindsight, this makes sense, and our society must understand these dynamics, especially when judging an officer's reaction to a lethal force incident as portrayed in the news.

What many in our society also fail to understand is that, when forced to choose, as was the case in a situation like our scenario, one person's safety is more important than the other person's safety. The officer in our scenario needs to protect his or her own life first. This was one of the messages of our training, and this message is preached to officers throughout their academy experience and recertification courses. We know almost nothing about this armed man, and this armed man can turn his weapon on the officer faster than the officer can react. As such, most police department policy manuals authorize the use of lethal force in this instance, even though the person in crisis is suicidal. Indeed, the philosophy of law enforcement reflected in most policy manuals is to first protect the innocent and bystanders; second comes the safety of the officer; third, when feasible, the safety of the actor/aggressor/perpetrator. It is very difficult to comprehend, but there are many cases in which a person in crisis lashes out at the people trying to help and save them. Drowning people can be dangerous because they will drown the people trying to save them, and it is not unheard of for suicidal people to kill others before killing themselves. Typical police department policy authorizes the use of lethal force in response to a situation like the one presented in our scenario, from the moment the officer sees the gun. Even with this policy in place, and with officers well-aware of their department's policy, only 28 percent of officers in our training shot the role player in our scenario, and some did not even draw their weapon when the gun was presented.

Our scenario-based training most often consisted of a group of about ten officers who went through our scenario one at a time. We then met as a group to debrief the experience. We showed the officers photos from the scenario, and their reactions were outstanding. The photos below got the most audible reactions.

This officer (on the right) did not have his weapon out, even though this stranger in front of him had his out. Could this officer draw his weapon, aim, and shoot the role player before the role player shot the officer? Is this a good time for this officer to gamble his life for a stranger in crisis? This officer is behind in the count and would not be able to catch up if the man in front of him decided to turn on the officer. Were our role player armed with a knife, this officer would clearly be in the danger zone and past the point of no return. Our role player is holding out his left hand, indicating to the officer not to come any closer and to stop what he is doing. This officer is being warned, yet is still trying to press ahead with trying to stop a suicide.

This officer's (on the left) attention is clearly on the weapon. How easily could our subject take his left hand and punch the officer in his head. The officer would never see it coming. It would be a much safer tactic to have the subject put his weapon on the ground and then back away. The officer in the scenario pictured above, as was the case in so many of the other times we ran our training scenario, commanded this subject to drop his gun. Our subject always disobeyed this directive.

How should this officer interpret the subject disobeying the command to drop the weapon? Does this disobedience indicate a higher threat to the officer? Is it wise for this officer to get so close to this person, or to let this person continue to close in?

And finally, one more example pictured below in two photos. The officer is on the left.

Even if there were no weapons present in this last scenario, is this officer allowing this stranger to get too close? In the last photo, it looks to me as if our subject is in a football lineman's stance, ready to jump off the line and engage the other team. Notice where the officer's weapon is and how easily it could be grabbed by our suicidal subject.

After showing these, and other photos, and allowing the officers to groan aloud and criticize, we showed them photos of how close they let their role player get to them. This perspective typically led to silence, or more groans. It was very difficult for officers to think through how to handle this situation. They wanted to help, and they surely did not want to kill. It was also difficult for them to remember precisely everything that happened, so having an outside perspective, like the one provided by actual photos, was a helpful and humbling training aid. Most officers walked away from the training with their eyes opened. They all could see that their humanity, their heart to help another person, could easily lead them to being in a situation that could kill them instantly. We wanted officers to be fully informed so they could make an educated and experienced choice if faced with something similar in the real world. We were not against de-escalation or negotiating. Both Sgt. Pierpoint and I have been negotiators for over 15 years, yet we are against trying to de-escalate/negotiate in a situation that is too dangerous for those responding.

In our post-training debriefing we also talked through what it is like for officers after being involved in a lethal force incident. Officers typically face an onslaught of pressures from the public (particularly in social media posts), their department's administration, the district attorney's office, a grand jury, the local and national media, co-workers, friends, and even family. Couple this with many officer's lack of access to competent, understanding, and trustworthy mental health support, and life can quickly feel out of control. With no place to psychologically process all that comes with killing another person, no matter how justified by law, policy, a supportive department, and even an understanding public, an officer can experience the lingering effects of this type of traumatic event, typically in the form of anxiety and/or depression.

How in the world is an officer to navigate all the forces, both internal and external (including the sometime vicious forces in our society, amplified by our media), after someone crosses the kill line? Training officers about what comes after a lethal force event can help prepare them to respond well to such an event itself, and for its aftermath. No one wants to kill, but far too often those in control (e.g. the man with the gun, knife, bomb, etc.) determine the outcome, and those of us coming to help are actually compelled by the demands of society to respond with force. According to Vince DalFanzo (retired FBI hostage negotiator), "We can tell people how to land the airplane, but they are the ones at the controls."

*****

About a year after holding these trainings for officers and deputies, every once in a while, an officer would approach me and thank me for the training. Then the officer would tell me a story about a call and the ways in which it was similar to the training experience. He or she would recount how being mentally prepared made all the difference, and how close he or she came to pulling the trigger.

CHAPTER THREE

WORKING WITH THE LUBBOCK COUNTY SHERIFF'S OFFICE

As iron sharpens iron, so one person sharpens another.
—Proverbs 27:17

The first full-scale callout I had with the Lubbock County Sheriff's office was in 2015, and is a great illustration of all the parts of a SWAT response working, and sometimes having difficulty working, together. Three people in a rural part of our area were having target practice on their property (it is Texas after all!). At some point, the subject of this callout pointed his weapon at the two people he was shooting guns with on his property. The dispute arose over who owned one of the guns, with the female of the group claiming it belonged to her deceased ex-husband. She got into an argument with the landowner, and then the male who was with them inserted himself into the dispute. Things escalated to the point where the male found himself at the wrong end of said weapon, and at this point the man and woman left the property to call the police. This call occurred in a small jurisdiction, so one officer responded. After this lone officer had a gun pointed at him, he retreated and called the county sheriff's office to assist. The county determined a SWAT response was warranted. A few years prior, I had joined their team as the psychological consultant, and now I got the honor of working with them for the first time.

The following events occurred prior to my arrival on scene. The target location was a house at the end of a 300-foot-long driveway. The property contained a few outbuildings and a couple of trees, but most of it was in the middle of a flat, open field. There were some other houses as close as 300 feet away, and deputies soon began evacuating these residences. SWAT team operators and their armored car (called a BATT for short) set up at the end of the subject's driveway with their weapons pointed towards the residence in the distance. Simultaneously, the negotiators began calling the residence and quickly established communication with the subject, whom we will call Bill. Bill was adamant that the police not set foot on his property. Over the course of this callout, Bill struck us as an anti-government type who was furious that things had escalated to the point of the SWAT team being called against him. The negotiator and her coach did an excellent job of allowing Bill to express his anger and sentiments while also explaining why the police were present. Soon, a state police helicopter arrived on scene and circled the property at a low altitude.

Bill then got into his car and attempted to leave his property. As he drove down his driveway towards the SWAT team, the state police helicopter dropped low in front of him and kicked up a lot of dust from the rotor wash. Bill decided to turn his car around and headed back to his house. He then got back on the phone with negotiators, and this was about the time I arrived on-scene.

I really wish I could have been there to watch the exchange between Bill and the state police helicopter, but, alas, I was home with my family. My parents were in town visiting, and my wife had scheduled family photos. About the time Bill was experiencing rotor wash, I was climbing in my car with my family and enroute to the photographer.

As the six of us turned out of our neighborhood, I got a call from Sgt. Brandon Pierpoint, the team leader for the negotiating team. My wife could tell from her seat way in the back of our car what was up. She could hear me saying things like, "Is he talking to us?" and "What's the tactical situation?" I heard my wife interject, from the third row of our car, "Turn the car around, Andy. Go do what you need to do." Usually when I'm doing things I'd rather not be doing (e.g. social situations that involve excessive small talk, grading papers, faculty meetings, etc.) I pray for a SWAT callout, but they rarely come in such a timely fashion. But in this case, the timing could not have been more perfect. Of course, I played it cool with my wife and insisted I continue on with them to family photos, instead of rushing off with the police to save lives. Right! In reality, I spun the car around like a scene from any good car chase movie, and bailed out of the car as it rolled past my house. I let the car keep going, knowing my family could certainly sort it out. I got in my car, obeyed all traffic laws, and was on-scene within seconds.

Unfortunately, I should've asked for the best approach route to the command post. Instead, I came across a LSO deputy blocking the road and pointing traffic another direction. I, however, knew I needed to go around the deputy to get where I wanted to be. We had ourselves a little standoff as I disobeyed his pointing and drove my car closer to him. He eventually came to my driver's side window and I got his permission to proceed, though without warning about where I was headed. I then drove right in front of the target residence. One of the SWAT members heard me coming, turned from facing the residence, and pointed his rifle my direction. He quickly recognized me, rolled his eyes, and went back to more important things than directing the mental health professional away from the danger zone. I was embarrassed, and hated the fact that my first callout with the LSO had begun with a mistake. I finally parked in a safer place and sought to find Sgt. Pierpoint, and restore my dignity.

As I put on my vest, I wondered if the helicopter overhead, and all the noise and tension it created, was making our subject tense as well. For me, and for negotiators, looking for a way to influence and change a situation is always in the back of our minds. I asked Sgt. Pierpoint about setting things up so our negotiator could offer to move the helicopter away. I later learned Bill was anti-government, so getting the state police helicopter to move back might serve to help Bill feel he had gained some power. My team leader understood my thinking, and asked me to share my idea with the SWAT commander.

I approached the SWAT commander, who was standing in a circle of brass (commanders), including the sheriff. He was very busy on the radio and consulting with his superiors regarding the situation at hand. I patiently waited for a break, then outlined my thinking to him, and asked if we could allow our primary negotiator, who I'll call Nina, to ask Bill if he would like her to move the state police helicopter away. The commander had been updated on the progress of our negotiations and knew Bill did not like anyone on his property, and did not like the government. However, the commander had to balance this against the likelihood of Bill getting in his car and trying to flee the scene again. Also of concern was the elementary school about 500 yards down the road. The commander was also considering moving the SWAT team onto Bill's property and getting them between Bill and his car. We all knew this move would infuriate Bill, would likely cause our negotiations to break down, and even incite Bill to violence. We wanted to deescalate this situation, but we also had to balance this with keeping the public safe and containing Bill, who was likely armed.

The commander listened to my idea and then asked about moving the tactical team onto Bill's land and getting between Bill and his car. Should we risk him trying to drive off again? Should we honor his request not to "trespass" onto his land and thereby keep negotiations going well? We talked it out and came up with a plan that tried to honor every element: Nina would offer to move the helicopter, and then, after orchestrating this for Bill, she would let him know that the SWAT team was going to have to move onto his property. Nina would then help Bill work through his anger and questions about this. Doing so would help Bill continue to see Nina as honest, helpful, trustworthy, and even help build rapport. The only problem with this plan was that tactical officers really do not like a bad guy knowing what they are about to do. In this case, however, SWAT was essentially in an open field, and Bill would see them coming down his driveway in an instant anyway. The tactical commander agreed with the plan and we set it in motion. Nina kindly offered to reduce the tension on-scene and assist Bill by ordering the helicopter to give Bill some space. Bill loved Nina's offer, so she had the helicopter rise to about 1000 feet. It became much quieter on scene, and I felt everyone relax. Nina then explained what the SWAT team was about to do, and why they had to do this. Bill used many colorful and passionate words to express his displeasure, and Nina allowed Bill to vent. It is easy to become defensive or to take such venting personally, especially when someone is directing their emotions at us. However, even when we are the object of someone's displeasure or wrath, we can still be nonjudgmental and listen respect-fully. We can give people the space to process their emotions, and even help them give language to what they are thinking and feeling. It is usually not helpful to explain ourselves at times like these, so the best option is to listen patiently and paraphrase the emotions thrown at us. Nina did this very well, which in turn helped Bill calm down a little. We then moved up the tactical team.

It seemed the negotiators and the SWAT team were able to both change the situation at hand, and react to it appropriately, but now we faced a new problem. Bill, who was very anti-government and anti-authority, now had the SWAT team on his front lawn. The SWAT team was now within voice range, and Bill unleashed his verbal wrath upon his new audience. The SWAT team responded by trying to reassure Bill at times, and give him advice at others. Bill was trying to bait them into a fight and was not talking with Nina. He was still on the phone with us, but his angry attention was on the BATT and the men with guns now on his property. Bill's goal was to make them look weak or bait them into a fight by provoking them. Nina did a good job of trying to get Bill to talk to her and focus on her, but this only lasted for short periods of time, especially because the men on the SWAT team were also negotiating with him. This was a problem because it divided Bill's attention and seemingly kept everyone from making any progress. The negotiating team leader talked with the tactical commander about this problem, and the commander was assured by his people that they were not talking with Bill. This was not confirmed by the negotiators, however, because we could clearly hear someone from the SWAT team talking with Bill. After several back and forth exchanges between the negotiating team leader and SWAT commander, eventually the order was given by the commander that no SWAT elements were to talk to our subject. Pretty quickly, Bill was again talking with Nina as he was before, and she began discussing with him a plan for coming out. Bill insisted that he had not intended for all this to happen. Nina played it cool and reassured Bill that everything would be okay. Bill then asked Nina if she would like him to make this callout last longer so she could get some overtime pay.

One of the goals of negotiators is to form a relationship with the person with whom they are talking. Negotiators want to understand the person, give them a chance to vent their emotions, and work with them to resolve the situation. Rapport is defined by Merriam-Webster's dictionary as, "a relationship characterized by agreement, mutual understanding, or empathy that makes communication possible or easy." My understanding of rapport also includes some type of bond, and even an ability to influence another person. My standard for rapport is pretty high, but I have found that this high standard is helpful to keep in mind when negotiating. If you try to influence someone or give them directions or suggestions without rapport, it generally does not go well. Conversely, if the person you are talking to is sympathetic to your plight as a single mom, which came up earlier in Nina's conversation with Bill, and asks if he can help you get some overtime, I think we have fulfilled my high standard for rapport. Nina and Bill were now on equal footing, and Nina could make suggestions to Bill about how to resolve this volatile situation. And for the record, in my 20 years of doing this, I've never heard an angry, anti-government type who was close to starting a gun fight with the SWAT team, soften to the point of asking the negotiator if he could help her out by extending a callout so she could get some overtime. This is rapport.

Bill stated that he would surrender himself to Nina, but not to any of those (censored) SWAT guys. Typically, negotiators do not use the term "surrender," but this was Bill's language. His goal was to make them look weak by letting Nina take him into custody. The negotiators loved this plan but, again, had to coordinate with the command and tactical members. This plan was not a normal way of doing things in a dangerous situation. Everyone was concerned about Nina's safety, even though she was a trained and experienced police officer.

Another factor in play here was how easily ego could become a part of the negotiation. Tactical and/or command staff could let their ego become a factor in their decision making and not want to give Bill what he wanted, especially because Bill could be quite disrespectful and was gifted at getting an angry reaction out of people. The SWAT team could also let ego become a part of things if they thought they should be the ones to talk with Bill, if they got angry and were baited into a confrontation, or if they just wanted to establish who was in charge. It's difficult to give something without a guarantee of receiving something in return.

The negotiating team was successful in selling the plan to have Bill taken into custody by Nina. The BATT was to come to the end of Bill's driveway, pick up Nina, and take her up to Bill's house. There Nina would exit, stand next to the driver's side of the BATT with another SWAT officer next to her, and Bill would come to her and be taken into custody. Normally, SWAT would take a dangerous suspect into custody, but command was willing to do this, in part because there were a number of SWAT members and snipers in position to protect Nina.

Nina, myself, a driver, and Sgt. Pierpoint (who picked up a rifle and sat on the back of our pick-up), loaded up and headed to the end of the 300-foot driveway. We waited, and waited, and then had a little trouble with our radios. Eventually, we learned that the SWAT team did not want to lose their tactical advantage by moving the BATT down the road to pick up Nina. So, instead, we were to drive down the driveway and park behind the BATT. We were on the phone with Bill as we learned this, and he objected to this change in plan. He then abruptly said he needed to talk to one of his friends and hung up on us as we were driving down his driveway. Nina called him back and was successful getting him on the phone about the time we were getting out of the pickup and into position to take him into custody. I climbed into the passenger seat of the BATT and had a loud hailer available to me in case it was needed. I knew from my time and experience with the Lubbock SWAT team that the last thing they needed was to have to worry about the mental health professional's location.

From my perch, high up in the passenger seat of the BATT, I watched as Bill walked towards Nina, and then saw the SWAT rescue team move up in an effort to cut off Bill from being able to retreat back into his residence. I did not expect this, and in that moment, I thought everything we had worked for over the last few hours was lost. When Bill saw the SWAT team move up, he lost his mind and started yelling at the rescue team, while also heading back towards his front door. It was obvious to everyone that Bill would beat the SWAT team to the door, so SWAT froze. Then Bill froze. We all held our breath as we watched this unfold. Everyone except for Nina, that is, who kept talking and worked to keep Bill's attention on her and off of the SWAT team. Eventually, Bill shifted his attention from the SWAT team, focused on Nina, walked towards her, and allowed her to put handcuffs on him as the SWAT team quietly stood ready. Whew! Bill got what he wanted, and we got what we wanted.

Throughout the last part of this negotiation, Bill periodically made vague threats (e.g. that armored car won't protect SWAT, this was a test...and this nagged at us). After we took Bill into custody, SWAT entered Bill's house to clear it and make sure it was safe. We watched them enter the house, then quickly evacuate the house. Apparently, earlier in the standoff, Bill had turned on the gas burners on his stove and lit candles throughout his living room. We deduced that when Bill realized Nina was coming up to the house to take him into custody, he went through the house and blew out the candles and turned off the gas. When SWAT entered his house, the smell of gas was still apparent, so they vacated. It seems Bill's earlier promises not to harm Nina were true, as were his threatening statements towards the SWAT team.

Bill harbored a lot of anger towards authority. His goal that day was to save face, and to make his adversary (the state and the SWAT team) "look weak." Had anyone's egos gotten involved, be it the sheriff, the SWAT commander, other brass on scene, Nina, myself, or Sgt. Pierpoint, I believe this callout would have ended very badly, and possibly in the explosion of Bill's house. An interesting side-note: Bill made bail the next day and went to breakfast. In the same restaurant sat two sheriff's deputies who had not been involved in the events of the previous day. Bill bought their breakfast as he left for home. I'm no psychologist, but I wonder if this, too, was another move demonstrating his power and benevolence.

*****

I would love to discuss all the things Nina did well in her negotiations with Bill and thoroughly analyze what she accomplished, but will only touch on this briefly. She employed all the basic active listening and rapport building skills, and did so very naturally, with authenticity and openness. She incorporated some advanced skills that, in my opinion, led to the peaceful conclusion of an easily volatile and deadly combination of factors. While humble, she did not give away her power; when Bill asked, in a way that seemed pushy and bossy to me, who was in charge, Nina answered, "I am in charge as far as things between us go.". Bill had a problem with authority, but also did not respect someone who would shy away from him. Nina was understanding, yet firm when needed. She was accommodating and without ego. She listened well, was conversationally generous (never interrupting), and appropriately humble. Nina earned a departmental meritorious service commendation for her work that day, and I was so glad to see her do so.

There were many difficulties our team had to overcome that day, and we could not have done so without working together. A short list of these difficulties:

1. Bill's demands that we not set foot on his property

2. Bill's innate ability to anger others and engage their ego (e.g. ordering the SWAT guys around, calling them "b----", and his great skill at arguing)

3. Bill's friends coming to the scene

4. SWAT talking to Bill while we were trying to talk to Bill (it is often hard to stay in one's lane and not work against each other)

5. Coordinating with the state police helicopter

6. What to do if Bill got in his car again

7. Bill's safety and rights, our safety (especially since Bill was armed), and the safety of the surrounding community

8. The overall stress of the situation and how that affected each individual on our team

9. The pressures placed upon law enforcement from society

10. Proper decision-making based on the facts at hand, and informed by careful listening to details while under stress (e.g. Bill made a number of vague and veiled threats throughout our negotiation with him).

What factors led to this callout with Bill and Nina going so well? One clear element in its success was Nina's individual skill. This was only one part of the entire operation, however, and could not have succeeded without all the others. For instance, when I arrived on scene, I had an overall perspective that those in the trenches may not have had. Individual members were focused on their tasks and on other parts of responding to this callout. SWAT was assessing the danger and possible responses, and patrol officers were determining how to evacuate innocent neighbors and contain the scene, while also considering how to respond to Bill's friends, who supposedly were on their way. Sgt. Pierpoint was coordinating personnel and getting resources to the scene while also relaying the information being acquired via Nina's conversation with Bill. The sheriff had his concerns, the SWAT commander his, and when I arrived, I took a minute just to get the overall feel of the situation. The helicopter was making me tense, so I thought of our subject and what he might be feeling, then learned of his attitude towards authority, and eventually made my recommendations. All these parts worked together to contain the scene, help lead to decisions regarding the best and safest response, and to a plan that Nina offered and articulated to Bill. One side note: Everything described here is but a snapshot in time from a three-hour crisis response.

So, what can be learned from this and how can it be applied? There were many components that contributed to our success. For us it started with team member selection, then training, working together, experience, and our personal characteristics (see Barrick and Mount, (2005) for more on personality and performance; see Yalom and Leszcz (2005) for more about group dynamics). Training is another component, and an example is training with scenarios and projects that are harder than what would typically be seen in day-to-day work. Another example is using exercises in which a team can practice working together (e.g. exercises that require planning, decision-making, collaboration, openness, conscientiousness, intuition, brainstorming, hearing and communicating the perspectives of others, working through problem-solving as a group, learning to trust each other, or learning each other's strengths, weaknesses, motivations, and pet peeves). An exercise that we use in our monthly negotiator training is to have one person with their back to another person, each in a chair. Each person is to argue one side of an issue (e.g. immigration policy, who the next president should be, why euthanasia or legalizing drugs is good, etc.). After both persons have communicated their respective sides thoroughly, they switch roles and argue the other persons' points. Another exercise we use is to have one person face away from another. The second person is seated at a table with the ingredients needed to make a peanut butter and jelly sandwich. The first person must describe in detail to the second person the step-by-step process for making the sandwich. This exercise typically ends with something less than a sandwich, and illustrates how difficult it can be to clearly describe a step-by-step task, such as how to put down a gun and exit a building surrounded by a SWAT team.

Another component needed for group success is each individual perfecting their own skills and becoming proficient at their job. They must also learn to regulate themselves, their emotions, and their reactions (see writing and research on Emotional Intelligence as another example). Doing so can also help build trust, and trust will be needed during the stress of an important or difficult project. Training together and experience working together help demonstrate the value of each person's perspective.

Then there's the skill of having an overall view of the situation at hand. Those in the trenches have their views and perspectives, and they need to be considered and taken into account. There is also the need to synthesize this information into a meaningful and useable whole. It is difficult to focus on a specific task while simultaneously considering all parts of a complicated mechanism. Once all the perspectives and elements are considered, a plan can be formulated and a decision made (see Boyd's OODA loop - Observe, Orient, Decide, Act as another resource related to these topics). In our case, we needed to find a way to help Bill save face, especially when it was easy to dislike Bill or feel like he was trying to push us around. General questions to ask in these instances are: What is our goal? Can we agree on the goal? What are we willing to sacrifice? Can we put pride and ego aside, and be humble and open as needed and for the accomplishment of a larger goal? Watching over our own pride and ego, not taking things personally, even when very passionate about what we see and need, are hallmarks of high-functioning individuals, teams, and companies. For negotiators in particular, the added quality of being empathetic and caring, even when someone is angry at you or trying to manipulate or deceive you, is indicative of skilled and successful negotiators.

You know a team is high-functioning when they can work well under acute or chronic stress, and are able to adapt/be flexible on the fly. Teams who can sensibly consider ideas and perspectives under stress and in crisis are able to cover all the angles, and this is something that must be practiced ahead of time. High-functioning and mature supervisors and managers are able to consider personality and decision-making styles, value the perspectives of others, and accept their limitations, all the while making room for the strengths of others. SWAT team commanders and business leaders can easily overlook the strengths and contributions of those they supervise, especially when under pressure, or when they forget that the strengths of others can complement their own. Though not perfect, nor always smooth, our callout with Bill, for me, represents our team working well together and covering all the angles, from individual proficiency, to team dynamics, personality, and decision-making.

*****

The SWAT and negotiating teams at the Lubbock County Sheriff's Office were asked to assist a police department about 45 minutes away from Lubbock with a murder suspect who was barricaded in a residence. When we arrived, a lone negotiator with this smaller department was on the phone with the suspect. This was his first negotiation. We set about supporting, coaching, gathering information, and eventually setting up the mobile command center. This new negotiator did a great job with a very difficult person who had very little to lose. We also had a new SWAT/Incident Commander for this callout. We had all worked together before, but the new commander was getting to experience the joys and pressures of handling a multijurisdictional event, including how costly an operation like this is, getting innocent neighbors out of harm's way, questions from his superiors, and trying to decide if force should be used versus continuing to negotiate with a barricaded murder suspect.

Negotiations continued for hours, and there were indicators of progress, including our subject calming, talking to us for longer periods of time, having a simple conversation, and talking to us about his crime. Our subject eventually started to sound sleepy! We put our heads together and decided that it was safest to have him go night-night. Our negotiator put on his late-night DJ voice, and acted as a great sedative. Soon we could hear the sound of heavy breathing, could see a long line of zzzzzz emanating from the target location, and were all convinced he was asleep. None of us had talked someone to sleep, aside from those of us who've had to put infants to bed, and it was quite surreal to do the same kind of thing with someone accused of murdering someone hours earlier. Our subject was taken into custody without incident. This was a great callout and conclusion to this incident for this new negotiator with whom we worked, and for our new SWAT commander. It was a test of how we would all work together, and in my opinion, set the stage for how we could work together on future callouts.

*****

In another callout, in a chaotic part of my city, the US Marshal's Office attempted to serve an arrest warrant on a man accused of the sexual assault of a child. For whatever reasons, the service of this warrant did not go as planned and the Marshal's Office contacted the Lubbock Country Sheriff's Office (LSO) for assistance. When I arrived, the Lubbock Police Department (LPD) was also on scene, so I felt like I was cheating on LPD as I walked around in my LSO uniform. I did, however, keep my LPD patches on my vest.

LPD negotiators who were working on patrol this day were already on this call, but LPD patrol commanders made the decision to pull them out because the Marshals called in LSO SWAT. Luckily, we are all professionals and work for the benefit of the emergency at hand, and not for glory or territory. Being concerned with territory or glory seems to lead to division, frustration, and losing sight of the goal. The LPD negotiators continued to assist the LSO negotiators because they were shorthanded. LSO negotiators began calling out to the subject, who was barricaded in a small apartment, while LPD negotiators interviewed some people involved.

I walked up to the residence and took my place near the primary negotiator as he called out to the man inside. It seemed there had been a little dialogue going, but not much more. The SWAT commander was getting his mind around the situation, and placing men and equipment as needed. He also had a couple of new SWAT operators, so he was teaching, mentoring, and reminding them of what was needed. To all be standing there together made communication easier, as we all attended to our different concerns and goals, the primary of which were our own safety and scene security.

It soon became clear that safety and communication with our subject would be improved if we all moved around to the back door. Shortly after we did this, our subject asked to speak to one of the Marshals. A guiding principle of hostage negotiating is to not switch out primary negotiators. Continuity, rapport building, not being manipulated, not losing anything that has been gained; all these are reasons to avoid switching negotiators. Even so, there are times in which switching out a primary negotiator is necessary, or even advantageous, such as very early on in a conversation, or after many hours because of negotiator fatigue. Switching out a primary negotiator with someone who is not a negotiator, however, is quite rare. In this case we considered this option because:

1. It was early in the callout and our primary negotiator did not have much dialogue with our subject

2. Our subject let us know that he had a preexisting relationship of trust with and was willing to talk to the Marshal he was requesting

3. We could easily trust that the Marshal would not work against us or make worse the circumstances at hand

4. The Marshal knew his way around a dangerous scene.

We were concerned about how coachable the Marshal would be, and if he had the basic characteristics one would want in a negotiator. We quickly learned that all of the above were present.

I took up the position of coach and teacher, and it was clear that this Marshal naturally had all the basic negotiator skills needed. He was calm, rational, listened well, was conversationally generous, and did not interrupt, was open to input from me and from our team, sounded empathetic and caring, and was collaborative with our subject. Here's what we looked like:

You can see our SWAT commander to my left, me in my vest and helmet leaning down with my hand on the Marshal, the SWAT team in front of me, and the Marshal on my right, speaking through the open door to our subject, who was barricaded in a bathroom and claiming to have a pistol. We could all easily hear each other and our subject. We could quickly work together to support the conversation the Marshal was having with our subject, and plan together with the other negotiators and SWAT elements. An added benefit was that the SWAT team could hear what we were saying and how we were talking to the subject. They could see if our conversation and tactics were working, and in this case, they were working very well. The Marshal made a few statements that got a good reaction from our subject, and head nods and looks of approval from the SWAT team.

Our subject soon had another demand: he wanted a cigarette. We asked how he would like the cigarette delivered, and he asked that we roll it under the closed door to his bathroom. I turned to the negotiators behind us and gave them my car keys. Because a demand for a cigarette had become a common request in recent LPD callouts, I was nominated to keep a baggy of cigarettes and a lighter in my car, partly because I was the least likely to steal one for myself.

The SWAT commander gave us a quick nod, and then discussed the delivery plan with his team. This quick agreement and access to a cigarette made our negotiations smooth and seamless, gave the subject the impression we were professionals who knew what we were doing, and helped reduce tension. A good negotiating policy is to give something in order to demonstrate our trustworthiness and character. Asking our subject how he would like the cigarette delivered demonstrated our respect for him and our willingness to be accommodating. We asked that he come out after he had his smoke and he agreed. We reviewed the come-out plan and his cigarette delivery plan. We also asked that he put down his gun, which he agreed to do. Everything was calm and the conversation the Marshal was having with the subject was reasonable and normal (aside from all the guns, body armor, and law enforcement). We were ready to deliver a cigarette, and were hopeful this would lead to the subject coming out of his bathroom peacefully. If you want someone to trust you, demonstrating your trustworthiness first goes a long way.

The SWAT team was ready and two officers with shields entered the apartment. The SWAT commander was among the other operators that entered and, after they reached the door of the bathroom (which was about eight feet from the outside door), the SWAT commander called an audible. The SWAT commander asked our subject to open the door. The Marshal gave me a look indicating his confusion about what was happening. I gave him a sheepish shrug and took my seat on the front row to find out what was going to happen. I tried not to wince, but I think the Marshal could tell I wasn't enjoying a sudden and surprise change of plan.

The SWAT commander asked our subject to open the door, and our subject was not having it. The commander tried once more, but then switched strategies and told him the cigarette was coming under the door now. Our subject calmed, the cigarette rolled, the team backed out, and the Marshal began speaking again. We were now back where we started and no damage was done by the seemingly sudden change of plan.

Our subject finished his cigarette and now it was time to see if he was a man of his word, and if all the effort and energy we'd invested to this point would pay off. It was clear he was still hesitant, so I encouraged the Marshal to review all we had done for our subject, how well things had gone, that our subject was a man of his word, and review what was going to happen once our subject exited the bathroom. The Marshal also added a little reality check; "You can't stay in that bathroom forever…" After about five minutes our subject calmly opened the door, showed us his hands, and walked out to us. Everything was calm, there was no shouting, and the Marshal peacefully put handcuffs on our subject. The SWAT team cleared the residence and all was secure. In about an hour we were successful in talking a man charged with the sexual assault of a child into handcuffs without anyone getting hurt. This Marshal conducted himself with calm and poise. He navigated the conversation peacefully, while also learning on the fly how SWAT and negotiators operated. Afterwards, I suggested to him that he was a natural negotiator and should consider joining up with a negotiating team as soon as possible.

A couple postscripts. Another job of a negotiator coach or supervisor is safety. Notice the placement of my hand on the Marshal's back in the next photo:

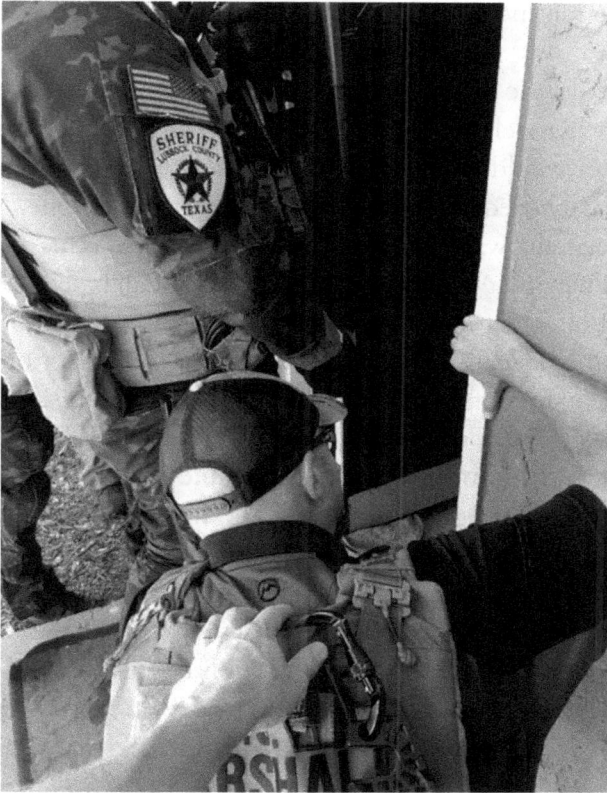

A normal human reaction when talking to someone in another room, and when you are trying to hear someone, and when you are focused and deep into a conversation, is to lean in. However, in this case, leaning in could lead to lead poisoning. As this man's coach, you should assist him in his conversation with our subject, coordinate with the other elements of our team, and make sure he stays safe. With regard to the latter, I had to pull him back a little, while also thinking ahead and trying to be ready for the unexpected. In this case, if things all of a sudden went horribly wrong, I was ready to pull this man out of the doorway and to my right. However, the negotiators on our team were stacked up to my right, assisting us with the conversation and providing us with information and a cigarette. You may have to remind your teammates that they need keep your avenue of egress clear.

Afterwards, the SWAT commander and I chatted about his calling an audible when delivering the cigarette. He said he just wanted to see if our subject would come out. He was ready to abandon his attempt as quickly as needed, and we all saw no harm was done. We would have appreciated a warning from him prior to giving this a try, but we understood why that wasn't possible. It's also not all bad to leave people room to try out their intuition.

It is impossible for one person to cover all the priorities faced in a SWAT operation, and so a dedicated and professional team of multi-taskers is required. Trust, being gracious to the other members of the team, and all working towards the same goal are what makes our SWAT and negotiating teams at the LSO and LPD high-functioning and effective when it comes to resolving highly volatile, dangerous, and potentially dangerous situations.

I wrote an article on this subject titled "US SWAT Operator Experience, Personality, Cognitive-Emotion Regulation and Decision-Making Style." This article can be found in *Policing: An International Journal, 41 (2),* 2018, pages 247-261. The full reference is available in the back of the book.

CHAPTER FOUR

CALLOUTS CLOSE TO HOME

When our team gets called into service, I typically have a very good response time, even though I'm in my private vehicle. This may be due to my driving very fast, keeping my gear in my car, and rolling down my window and howling loudly at every red light. So far, I remain speeding ticket-free. The story of my closest call will be detailed in chapter six.

I am often asked if I am ever afraid about my safety or if I carry a gun. The answer to both is no. One reason is because I am surrounded by highly-trained professionals, which makes these callouts some of the safest places in town. Another is because I have almost zero firearms training. Lastly, LPD was gracious and supportive enough to give me a vest and helmet. I'm such a nerd that I will put it on at home when my children won't eat their dinners. Any excuse for putting on my vest and helmet will do! Here's a photo of my beloved gear for your home photo album.

I think my perspectives on safety and fear are also influenced by my work providing assistance to those who have just suffered a traumatic event. Victims' questions are often about their fear concerning their future safety. How could something like this hit so close to home? I am also not afraid while at home, even though I have seen many examples of trauma and calamity that have occurred in someone's residence. Fear should rarely be associated with a location, but rather, a healthy caution toward the people involved. I have had a few calls in my neighborhood, but believe I am safe even so.

As coordinator of our Victim Services Crisis Team, I don't go on as many calls as I once did. It's difficult, and even disrespectful to someone with whom I'm speaking to be busy with one call and then step away to coordinate another. Even so, every once in a while, the stars align and I put on my dusty Crisis Team jacket and head out. One such occasion was when LPD dispatch called regarding a deceased person. The house number was the same as my own, and the street was two streets over. I could have walked to the scene in three minutes. There was also no one else on the team available at that time, so off I went.

I walked into a house much like my own. In the kitchen, an older gentleman of middle-Eastern descent lay on his back, deceased. I met two young officers for the first time, who gave me a quick overview. The deceased was the patriarch of this family, and there were four generations in and around the home. In the back bedrooms were some grandchildren and great-grandchildren who were grieving. Many of the men were outside and in the living room. The family physician was also there. The officers were concerned about the son of the deceased because he was agitated and seemed not to understand why the officers were keeping he and his family away from the body of their loved one. The officers wanted me to check on the grieving children, and to check in with the son, who apparently was now the new patriarch of this family.

I walked over to a group of men who appeared angered by my presence. One of them stepped forward and got into my personal space. I introduced who I was and my role there, and asked him if he had any questions or if there was anything I could do. He pressed in to within inches of my face and asked with subdued, yet angry, passion, "Why can we not be with my father?" I made a calculation in the moment… and decided that the best and most respectful thing I could do was to neither be fearful, nor back away. Standing my ground, I looked him directly in the eyes and, as compassionately as possible, explained why the officers were doing what they were doing. Primary in this was to preserve things as the officers found them so the Medical Examiner's office could clearly determine why this death occurred. I explained that, when a death occurs outside of the hospital, these officers had a duty to be careful, thorough, and treat every death investigation the same. The man, inches from me, seemed to understand, but then also expressed his heartfelt desire for his family to perform a ritual around the deceased. I asked him if this ritual would include touching the body, and he assured me it would not. I left him for a few moments to speak with the officers and to see what they, and the Medical Examiner's office would be comfortable doing.

I was worried these new officers I did not know would be hard-liners and decline my request, but was pleasantly surprised that they were okay, as long as no one touched the body. I let the man know everything was ready, and he gathered his family. The two officers and I stood aside and respectfully watched as this family encircled their deceased patriarch, played a song in a language I did not know, and rotated the circle around so each member had time at his head. Soon, the ritual was over, and shortly thereafter the Medical Examiner's van arrived to claim this man's body.

These were new experiences for me. I had never seen a ritual like this, nor had interactions with someone as I did with that man that night. It was an honor to witness this family paying their respects to their loved one in a way I'd never known, and standing with the officers as it occurred was also an honor. For us to be open to the needs of others, even when we do not understand them, is a mindset and skill that's developed consciously and over time. The benefits of this mindset, both to others and for ourselves, can be surprising.

*****

On another occasion, we had a SWAT callout about the same distance away from my home but in another part of my neighborhood. My response time was stellar, and I soon got to don my vest and join the other negotiators as they talked with the woman, who had called 911. The woman and I instantly recognized each other because we'd gone to college together, and she was good friends with my wife. I think she was both relieved and embarrassed to see me, but it was hard to say for sure. She reported that she and her husband had been fussing, and the argument had escalated to where he had pulled a weapon on her. She left the house quickly, but the children were still inside. Through the course of this tense event (tense for all of us because we had two children inside as potential hostages) we worked to gather information, calm my friend, and make a plan with her and the SWAT team.

The SWAT operators quietly surrounded the house as we worked with my friend to see about contacting her children and determine if they could exit the residence without detection or escalation. Soon my friend was able to text her son, who then woke her daughter, and the two of them were able to exit the house through the open garage door my friend had fled through about an hour prior. The children reported to us that their father was asleep on the couch. We all decided that the best thing to do was to leave this man alone in his home and allow him to sleep it off. They all had a place to stay, and we then planned to meet my friend in the morning so she could get her things and move out.

The next morning, two negotiators, me, my friend, and her two children arrived at the residence and the officers made contact with her husband. It was a simple exchange, but sad for everyone involved. We stood by, in case there was drama or danger, as my friend and her children gathered what they needed, and said very little to the man. It's sad to see what unresolved emotional and relationship issues, coupled with alcohol, can lead to. But even so, my friend was very good to all the officers involved and thanked us. It is always a sad thing to handle a situation as well as can be, yet conclude without a complete and fully positive resolution. It is tough to accept our limitations, especially when our compassion wants so badly to fix things.

*****

Lastly, there have been a couple times when I didn't even have to leave my house to assist with a SWAT callout. I'll include these two quick stories because I'm going to count them as happening in my neighborhood since I never left my house. The downside of these stories is that I never got to put on my vest, so I'm going to pause and look at it again.

In one case, I was consulted by a jurisdiction working a callout about a 90-minute drive from my house. Officers had chased a suspect into a house, and now had a hostage situation to navigate. They wanted to know what to do about all the family members and friends who were texting their barricaded subject. Their callout was further complicated by all the different agencies involved in responding, and because there was almost a friendly-fire incident. One of the officers from one agency almost shot an officer from another agency. I suggested they bring all the family to the scene, put as many negotiators as possible with each family member, and try to coordinate their messages to the subject. I figured a consistent message, one that mirrored what the negotiator was saying to the subject, would help calm the situation and might even help resolve it peacefully. Surprisingly, all the people texting the subject were agreeable and came to the scene. They were helpful and coachable, and the incident resolved soon after with the subject peacefully coming out the front door.

In the other case, I was sleeping peacefully in my bed and got to assist the FBI with a callout they were involved with in Missouri. A negotiator I had met at a conference a few years prior called me for consultation on their callout, to talk it through and see if they'd missed anything. A police officer who was armed with a pistol was barricaded in a hotel room with her children. These factors made this a very stressful situation for everyone responding to assist. This situation went on for so long that the first team of negotiators and SWAT officers had to switch out so they could rest, and now my friend and her FBI team had been at it for hours. They were at a dead end with their negotiations because this subject was non-responsive. Their concern for the children, the tactical limitations, the history of the officer involved, and the pistol kept everyone on high alert. As we talked it through, it seemed they had covered all the bases and tried everything we could think of. They had very little to work with, but even so, they were determined to do everything they could to help everyone in that hotel room. I wished her well and we hung up.

As you can imagine, going back to sleep after a conversation like this is not easy because my mind continued to search for ways to resolve this callout. I prayed for all involved, and was really hoping my friend and her team would not suffer losses like my team and others across the nation occasionally suffer. Forty-eight hours later I learned that this incident resolved peacefully. My friend's team was there so long that another team came in to relieve them. They had done all they knew to do, and now it was time to hand things over to a fresh and rested team. One of the children eventually unlocked/unbarricaded the door and escaped. The officer was taken into custody without incident, and hopefully received the personal help needed.

Being a dedicated and devoted negotiator comes with some pitfalls, not the least of which are having trouble knowing when to ask for outside help, when to seek consultation, and when to hand over a situation to another group of negotiators. Even though we all know that our capabilities are quickly diminished when fatigue sets in, making the decision to ask for help is still a hard one.

CHAPTER FIVE

FUN WITH SWAT

The SWAT team is there to react to a situation. Negotiators are there in the hopes of changing a situation.

It is becoming a standard of practice in the United States for negotiators to be sent out with the SWAT team every time they are activated. I agree with the notion that it is better to have on-scene what is needed, rather than trying to play catch up and getting resources to a scene after they're required. When I'm able, I join our negotiators when they are sent along on any high-risk warrant services the SWAT team is conducting. These warrant services typically begin with everyone involved gathering for a briefing. If the state police, homicide detectives, narcotics officers, or other squads are involved, they will join in the briefing along with the SWAT team, commanders, and negotiators. There have been times when more than one SWAT team, agency, and other additional resources are needed, so the room can get crowded.

In one example of a successfully executed warrant service, and as the bad guys were in handcuffs and their residence was being searched, an angry crowd gathered. I'd attended a couple of trainings on the topic of using negotiators to help with angry crowds, protest movements, and the like, and was hoping maybe I could use some of what I learned. A woman became very vocal and combative because she knew a baby was in the house. When an officer walked outside with the baby, she became very animated. I approached her and asked if I could do something to help resolve things. She wanted to take custody of the baby, so I approached some officers to see what could be done. She was allowed to walk closer to the residence, and the bad buys immediately recognized her. We all chatted and then obtained permission to give the child to the woman, along with some necessities. This served to resolve the situation for the moment.

About 20 minutes later, some yelling began in the crowd and quickly escalated into pushing and shoving. SWAT officers walked over and stood like soldiers between the two factions of this crowd. There was a lot of name-calling and many accusations flying back and forth, and the woman from earlier was in the thick of it. When I approached, she recognized me and explained the source of the drama. I asked where the baby was and who was taking care of it, and this seemed to divert her attention from the argument at hand. I asked if it would be okay if she left this fight for another day, and she agreed to do so. Her faction left the area and things calmed again. It's amazing how quickly a situation can escalate, and how quickly it sometimes can be defused.

*****

On another occasion, I arrived at the briefing early. My friend Colin was in charge of the planning and execution of this operation, and was preparing his briefing. I knew my role, yet playfully asked if I could be on the entry team today, and he laughed as he put my name in the run order for the team making entry into the house.

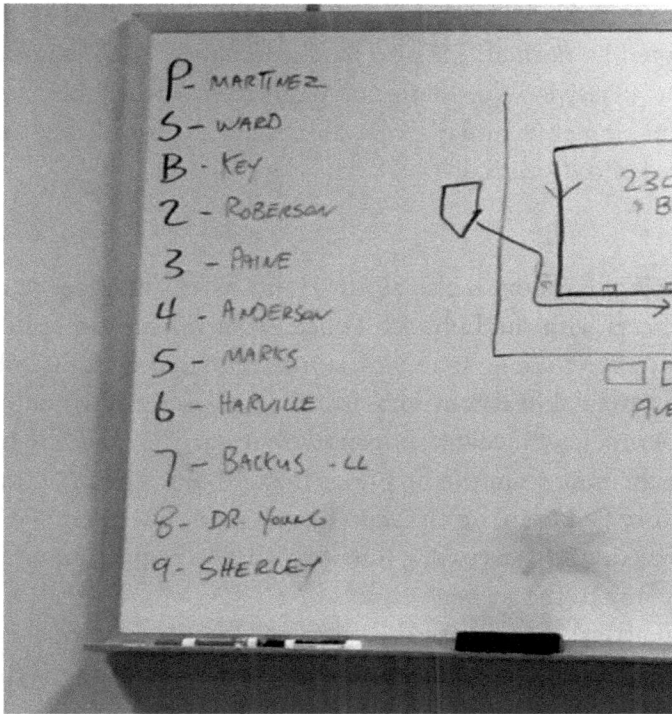

Of course, I snagged a photo and then sat quietly watching as other SWAT members, commanders, negotiators, and tactical medics walked in and took a look at the run order. The best part was when Nathan (the captain over the negotiator team) came in, looked at the board, gave a puzzled look, and continued on. The briefing started and Colin casually announced the run order. It seemed as if the rest of the room was in on the joke, or simply accepted that I'd be making entry with everyone today. I watched Nathan look out over the room in shock as everyone continued on as normal. Finally, he broke and leaned over to the SWAT commander and asked a question with a confused look on his face. The SWAT commander, who hadn't objected yet, gave an animated response (no way!) and Nathan gave a sigh of relief. On-scene, and after the warrant had been served, Nathan came over to me and chuckled as he recounted his inner disbelief at everyone seemingly going along with this plan and being totally flummoxed by this being accepted as normal. He also laughed at the SWAT commander's quick and decisive "No, that's not happening!" when Nathan asked if I was making entry today. Some things are so absurd they are easily overlooked and dismissed!

*****

The following story is also absurd, but was much harder to dismiss. Patrol officers with the Lubbock Police Department were called to an apartment after a young man, apparently impaired by some substance and with a mental health history, had fired a weapon. Arriving officers set up a perimeter, evacuated surrounding residences, and attempted to talk with the man from the first floor living room. The man was in his second-story bedroom, up the stairs and around the corner. SWAT was soon notified, and I excitedly, but with all due respect for traffic law, made my way to the scene.

Upon arrival, I met with the other negotiators from our team and got permission to join the negotiators who were already on the stairs trying to reason with our subject. I already had my vest and helmet on and was escorted down the alley, through a back garage that had about five patrol officers in it, through a small backyard, and into the living room of this two-story, four-room apartment. Negotiators were on the stairs, and we could all hear the erratic speech and paranoid movements of our guy. He was polite, as was our negotiator, Bryan, and it seemed the tone of the dialogue was promising, even though our guy was erratic. Bryan reassured our subject, while also helping him understand that he could not fire his weapon anymore and needed to come downstairs. Kimberlee was his coach and was on the stairs with Bryan. There were members of the SWAT team both in front of and behind them, and the ones in front had a ballistic shield. I think everyone in that room was a bit tense due to the erratic and unpredictable nature of our armed and mentally impaired subject, and because he could fire his weapon through the floor and easily hit one of us. Kimberlee and I worked to support Bryan's conversation, and give him as many useful ideas as we could create. After I'd been there about 20 minutes, it became clear we were going to be here a while due to our subject being difficult to convince, and who had a hard time concentrating on the issue at hand. We also had trouble hearing him.

We all agreed that backing out of the apartment would be wise, mostly because the man upstairs could fire through his floor and hit any of us. Bryan, Kimberlee, Tim (negotiator supervisor), and I all backed out, as did the SWAT team. Just as Bryan headed down, our subject slammed a door. Bryan told us later that the sound scared him and almost caused him to fall down the stairs. He played it cool at the time, so no one noticed. Bryan, Kimberlee, and I headed to our command unit to try and reestablish a dialogue with our guy, and began settling in for what could easily be a long and difficult conversation.

Thank you, Olivia, for taking this photo and capturing my helmet hair!

We got set up, and if memory serves, we also tried and failed to get our guy to talk to us on the phone. Soon Tim called Bryan back up to the residence, and Bryan and Tim attempted to talk to our subject from outside the residence using a bullhorn. They could see our subject in his room, and Bryan had some conversation with him. Bryan told me later that he had a history with this guy and he had recognized Bryan. Bryan also mentioned that, while talking to our subject about his girlfriend, the guy asked Bryan, "Did you ever get a chance to get with her?" Bryan said it was a little hard to come back from that comment. Overall, it seemed to Bryan and Tim that the conversation was heading in the right direction, but I was less convinced due to 1) his history of a psychotic disorder, and 2) his impairment due to some substance. It was true he was doing better and probably coming down from his high, but never forget that a Psychotic disorder has a much longer shelf life. We saw the extraordinary effects of a Psychotic disorder during our callout on the overpass with Colter, and here it was again.

The SWAT commander and Nathan asked me what I thought, and I shared my opinion that we were probably going to be there a while, even though our subject gave some impressions that he might come out peacefully. He gave Bryan and Tim a ten-minute deadline for coming out, and they relayed this to us over the radio. Bryan reviewed the plan and procedure for exiting his bedroom, and he seemed to mostly understand and comply. This was followed by our subject leaving the bedroom window and being non-communicative for a number of minutes. Bryan kept talking, reassuring and emphasizing to our subject the best and peaceful way to wrap up our situation.

A few minutes later we all got a report over the radio from the SWAT team that our subject was in custody. We were a little perplexed by this because our subject had been silent for so long, but assumed he'd walked out of his bedroom and was taken into custody, just as Bryan had suggested to him. But alas, our impaired subject had other ideas, as evidenced by the following photos:

We had learned earlier in the callout that the attic above our target bedroom opened up into a space that spanned the entire apartment complex. Anyone who gained access to the attic could crawl across the length of the building and access any apartment. Our subject knew this as well, and, during his little break from his conversation with Bryan, had scurried up into the attic and tried to make his escape. Fortunately, he didn't know how to safely crawl through the attic and promptly fell through the ceiling. His timing and location were perfect, as he used the SWAT team to break his fall. He was quickly taken into custody and was unharmed by his journey back to Earth.

It is worth noting that, in my experience and the experiences of many other negotiators with whom I have spoken, it is the very rare occasion when a subject gives a negotiator a long timeframe (e.g. longer than ten minutes) for surrender and actually follows through. It is more often the case that a subject is using that timeframe for other, typically nefarious, activities. It is also worth noting that apartments and homes where drug use is known to occur, often are decorated for Christmas year-round!

CHAPTER SIX

THINGS THAT MAKE YOU GO, HMM?

Sometimes crying or laughing are the only options left,
and laughing feels better right now. — Veronica Roth

For almost 20 years I have been part of a regional Critical Incident Stress Management (CISM) team comprised of officers, firefighters, medics, dispatchers, and mental health professionals from the Lubbock area. This team typically gets a few calls a year from the small towns and rural departments within a 300-mile radius of Lubbock. We also get called to the larger towns every once in a while, especially when there is a large-scale incident, such as the Walmart mass-casualty incident in El Paso, or the active shooter incident in Midland/Odessa. Our team will respond to assist first responders and give them an opportunity to psychologically process traumatizing events, and to show our support for them during difficult and trying times.

On one such occasion we were called to a small town about an hour away from Lubbock after local police, fire, and EMS responded to a shooting with multiple injuries/fatalities. Everyone knows everyone in a small town, so a tragedy like this affects everyone deeply.

This includes the emergency services people, many of whom, often, are volunteers. These responders frequently know the people they are called in to protect and help, and that was the case on this call.

When the call went out for a shooting with multiple injuries and an armed subject on the loose, everyone responded. Officers within this small department responded both to the scene and to calls identifying the shooter and his location in the small downtown area. They quickly found and confronted him. The shooter threatened to harm *them* as well, and when he pointed his gun at them, he was shot. The shooter continued to resist and had to be shot again, this time fatally. This department was quickly overwhelmed by two crime scenes and multiple injuries/fatalities to people they knew.

The chief of this department and I are long-time friends, so he called me soon after and asked our CISM team to come to his town that evening. I mustered a team, including Kimberlee and Zach from the CISM team at LPD. We divided the emergency responders into two groups, police in one, and fire and EMS in another. Matt, from the Lubbock Fire Department, and other members of his team took the fire/EMS group, and those of us from LPD took the group of police officers. We followed the "Mitchell model" of doing CISM and gave everyone a chance to psychologically process their experiences and emotions via questions we posed to the group. We asked people to tell us what happened from start to finish, to talk about the things they kept thinking about after the call was over, to tell us about the worst part(s) of this call, and to share any symptoms they might be experiencing. As best our team could tell, both groups benefitted from the opportunity, and hopefully would return to their "normal" more quickly than they would have without this purposeful opportunity to make sense of a traumatic event.

Our team met as a group to debrief each other before heading home. Listening to the traumatic events experienced by other people can also bother those trying to help, so supporting each other and giving each other a chance to decompress is also a good standard of care for a CISM team. It's also good to review how our meeting went, and how we might do better in the future. Afterwards, around 10 p.m., Zach and Kimberlee rode with me back to Lubbock. It was nice to talk things over together, see what stood out to each of us during our meeting, and have a laugh. It had been a long day for me prior to this call to assist, so I was ready to get some sleep, especially in light of my impending workday. I used all of this to rationalize my speeding, and it was working until a Texas state trooper lit me up and pulled me over. In college, during my trips between Lubbock and Abilene, I had been pulled over a time or two, especially because the national speed limit at that time was 55 m.p.h. In Lubbock, over the last 30 years, I'd been pulled over a couple times as well. In one case, it was two in the morning and I was stopped on a major thoroughfare by an LPD patrolman. I pulled over and looked through my rearview mirrors intently, trying to see who'd pulled me over. The LPD officer cautiously approached my car as I kept looking in the mirrors to see who it was. He slowly walked up my driver's side, and I noticed he was "slicing the pie" as he looked around my doorframe. Slicing the pie refers to carefully making one's way around a corner, ready to meet a threat. I then realized that he was quite worried about my behavior and what I was doing, or about to do. He slowly came around my doorframe and we made eye contact. "Dammit, Andy! You scared me!" I knew this officer well, but had no idea my actions had put him on alert. He quickly explained to me that someone furtively looking in their rearview mirror is a sign that they may try to run or fight. I quickly apologized, and we had a good laugh.

Back to the story at hand.

In this case, Zach, Kimberlee, and I were on the side of the highway, awaiting the trooper's walk up to my car. Zach and Kimberlee were very concerned, and this surprised me. Neither had been pulled over before, and both were quite nervous about how this was going to go. Kimberlee was in my passenger seat, atwitter about not wanting to get in trouble, and Zach was in my backseat exclaiming, "But I have a pistol on me!" It's a good thing I'm a crisis counselor and hostage negotiator; so I reassured them that I had this and they had nothing to worry about, and that I enjoyed how life had given me an opportunity to practice negotiating. I did not, however, have time to mock them about being police officers yet not knowing how a traffic stop was going to go! I guess it is better to give than to receive a traffic stop.

It has become second nature to me, over time, to coordinate or manage multiple crises at once. This case was just funny, but it does bring to mind how life's problems and stresses are often not just about one event. I had been up all day, tried to help people who were hurting and traumatized, and now had my own, personal crisis on the side of the highway. It is easy to get overwhelmed and angry when life piles on. I have often gotten snippy and short with loved ones when I had to go from one crisis to another. It takes practice to manage your own emotions and keep a proper perspective when everything around you has been stressful, tiring, and traumatic. Slowing down, taking one thing at a time, letting down and processing what just occurred when able to do so, and not allowing the emotions from one instance influence the next situation takes conscious effort and practice.

I keep my vest, helmet, go-bag, and all my outfits for callouts in my car.

I might strategically hang my shirts and jackets in the rear windows, just in case of moments like this one, and I watched the trooper through my side mirror peer into my back window and see my "Lubbock County Sheriff, SWAT" shirt. I let Kimberlee and Zach know the trooper was approaching and they quieted. I put my hands on the steering wheel and awaited my fate, still chuckling internally about having to calm the police officers in my car.

The trooper came to my window and asked me if I knew how fast I'd been going. I told him I did, and he asked where we were coming from. I told him the small town we'd just left, and he asked me what we'd been doing there. I started to tell him that we'd been there to assist the first responders after the officer-involved shooting they'd just had, but the trooper finished my sentence for me. He encouraged me to slow down and wished us a nice night. I turned to Kimberlee and Zach with a smug look of pride, and they extolled my skills as a negotiator and how I was able to talk myself out of a ticket in three sentences.

*****

Here's another old picture of me in a vest for your home photo album. This was after my first time on the range shooting with a pistol. Good thing I don't have to depend on my physical skills to make a living.

CHAPTER SEVEN

AUTHORITY AND FORCE

...understanding the fact that law is not enacted for the righteous person [the one in right standing with God], but for lawless and rebellious people, for the ungodly and sinful, for the irreverent and profane, for those who kill their fathers or mothers, for murderers...—1 Timothy 1:9 AMP

How much force should be used in this case?

Would the amount of force you might recommend in this case change depending on why this man was on this roof? Would the amount of force you recommend change if this were your roof? Would it change depending on what you knew about this man?

We often see a few seconds or minutes of a video depicting police use of force. In some cases, it is clear to all involved that a mistake was made on the part of responding officers. In the majority of cases, however, the answer is not so easily discerned, yet that does not stop people from making their own judgments. It is a shame that we expect grace from those judging us, but are free to be harsh when judging someone else. But I digress.

As you can see from the photo, these two officers are using as little force as possible. Would this be appropriate if this man had just stolen someone's mail? What if he had just committed a burglary? A murder? A rape? Would your opinion change depending on how long this had been going on? How long do we give this man to make a good decision? An hour? A day? What if he was suicidal and had not committed any criminal act? At what point should we escalate our use of force? How much should we accommodate him or give him in order, hopefully, to persuade him to make a good decision?

My thoughts, after doing this for over 20 years, usually begin with the same philosophy; I like to give something to get something, and I like to assume the best when appropriate. Others have been more punitive and expect this man to do what we want without question. Still others prefer him to give us something before we accommodate him. I would counter, what does it cost us to do something simple in order to demonstrate our trustworthiness and care? I like to show good faith by giving when we can and accommodating requests when it can be done safely and simply. This is because we are intervening with a stranger who knows nothing about us and is probably suspicious of our motives and character. When a scene is more complex or dangerous, however, these questions become more difficult to answer.

This work often reminds me of parenting young children. Children, and even the children I used to take care of at the Children's Home, need someone who can be stable when they are emotional. When an adult can go the extra mile, when situations allow, and show grace, trustworthiness, peace, and calmness, and help them work through their emotions or problems, things usually go smoothly and are resolved as quickly as possible. Parenting is an art that requires selflessness and empathy. It also requires discipline and boundaries, when appropriate. Too bad the SWAT team isn't on standby at my house when my children lose it.

Part of my job as a psychological consultant on the SWAT team is to give my professional opinion about the level of risk (harm to self or others) a person poses, and sometimes give my thoughts about the most appropriate way to respond to that level of risk. In the case shown in the photo above, our estimation was that this gentleman posed a low risk to self and others, aside from being armed with a knife. Because of the knife, we had to be sure some of the officers on the perimeter had their weapons drawn and ready at any moment, should the situation deteriorate. We based our overall assessment of this subject on his conversation with us. He became calmer and rational over time, even though impaired by a substance; he stopped jumping from roof to roof, and he never threatened anyone with the knife. He responded well when we fulfilled some of his requests (e.g. moving some uniformed officers back/out of view), and he responded well to our primary negotiator, Tino.

Tino offered him some water, and he accepted. Tino tossed it up to the roof, but his throw came up short. The subject reached out to grab it, teetered a little, but kept his balance. Tino tried again and all was well. So, when he told us he would drop his knife and come down if he could see his girlfriend, we entertained his request. Tino let him know the situation was too unpredictable for us to bring her up to the house, but after getting clearance from Nathan (our team commander and ranking officer on-scene), he could talk to her before we all left the scene and he went to the hospital. This wasn't good enough because he was somewhat paranoid and still distrustful. We suggested we could put his girlfriend in view of him, down the street. He eventually agreed, so we set about trying to facilitate the plan.

We had other negotiators with the girlfriend down the street, and they now had a good feel for her and how cooperative she would be with us. After talking with them on the radio, I walked over to their location and we chatted about the plan. These negotiators believed she would do well, even though she, too, was impaired. I then went about scouting out a good spot for the girlfriend and our guy on the roof to have a little eye contact from a distance. A couple of medics were also on scene, and they wear red shirts, so I asked one to join me. I hollered at our negotiator on the radio and asked if he could see me and the red-shirted medic. He could, and I could see him ask our guy on the roof if he could see us, too. He made eye contact with us and I asked our negotiator over the radio to ask our guy if he would like his girlfriend to stand in this spot for a moment. We soon got the go-ahead, and I went to fetch the girlfriend. Another aside…notice the way in which we orchestrated things here. We *asked* our guy if he would like his girlfriend to stand in that spot for a moment. In my view, this was a respectful way to interact with this man, and honored any sense of control or autonomy he might need or value.

As the girlfriend and I walked over to our spot, a gaggle of medics and firemen had gathered there. I waved them all away, but as we approached the spot another fire truck crept its way down the street and stopped right in my line of sight! I politely went over and asked the driver to back up, which he did. Now we were all set for this impaired woman and her impaired boyfriend/husband to have their moment, which they did. I escorted her back down the street, and our negotiator went over the come-down plan with our guy. He soon jumped down and was peacefully taken into custody. We took him to an ambulance that was waiting down the street, and we gave him and his girlfriend time to exchange hugs and professions of love and support as he lay on the EMS cot in handcuffs.

This was the first negotiation for Tino, and he did very well. He quickly developed rapport with our guy, and his approach was the right combination of firmness and empathetic accommodating. The team did a good job of supporting him, and his coach (Mike, the officer standing behind him) did a great job, too. This was Mike's first callout as a coach, and he did not like how close he and Tino were to an armed man in an elevated position. As we saw in chapter two, action beats reaction, and this unpredictable man easily could have stabbed both of our officers. They both had to trust that the officers behind them would be able to stop any threat on their lives. Tino and Mike sacrificed their safety in a very unpredictable situation, in the hopes of resolving it peacefully. It is great to watch all the officers on scene working as a team and all working towards the same goal in such a smooth, calm, and professional fashion.

*****

It is not an easy thing to properly respond to a crisis situation, especially when the primary tool is the use of force and taking control of a situation. LPD patrol officers were called to a shots-fired situation, and quickly determined from the family members involved that a SWAT callout was necessary. The man inside had fired his gun into his ceiling while fighting with his wife. He had been drinking and had a history of being volatile while impaired. SWAT, negotiators, and all of our equipment arrived and set up. We tried to contact the man while SWAT contained the situation and patrol officers evacuated the surrounding homes. I spent a lot of time talking with the family, and they were of the opinion that the police should leave and allow the husband to sleep it off. Our concern was for the welfare of the family, and the neighborhood, and we had to balance this with the lethality of the situation at hand and the family's input and wishes.

After a couple hours trying to contact the man without response, it seemed to us that the dangerousness and lethality of the situation were lowering. The family reported that this man had a history of sleeping it off and having a very different disposition upon waking. The family seemed amenable to leaving the area for the night so that they would be safe, and we would be able to leave a couple of patrol cars on the street and in the alley in case things unexpectedly flared up again. This seemed to strike the balance of not escalating the situation with this drunk man while also protecting the family and the neighborhood.

It was at this point that an old commander from another division stopped by the scene. Because he was now the ranking officer, technically he could call the shots and was in charge. He made the comment that he had not been to a SWAT callout in ten years and that they'd have kicked in a door by now. This gave us all pause, and we respectfully explained our estimation of the situation, the risk involved, and the best course of action given everything we knew. The commander could see our reasoning, especially the point we made about there being no major arrestable offense here, but was also worried about how the chief might react if we were wrong. We assured him that we would explain ourselves to the chief if needed, and that seemed to suffice. The big question for us was whether we should get into a gunfight with a man sleeping in his own home who was, at most, guilty of discharging a firearm within city limits.

We spoke with the family and everyone was good with our plan. It had been almost three hours since anyone had heard from the drunk husband, so it seemed the crisis had passed. It was a little surreal to watch everyone pack up and walk away from what had started as a very tense and chaotic call. There is always that feeling of, "We have to do something, we must take action," but that feeling is sometimes a mirage. In this case, it was our view that doing nothing was the best thing to do, and would certainly not escalate the situation into something lethal.

Just because someone has the power or authority doesn't mean they should use it, be it the power that comes from gun ownership, or money, or resources, or the authority that comes from being in charge of a business, government, or from being a parent. The purpose of power or authority is to find the best thing for all involved, from the home, in line at the store, in politics, or in these cases of law enforcement and crisis response. The use of power and authority is for the good of the individuals involved, and those more broadly affected by the situation at hand. Finding the balance of what is best for all involved is often a team effort. It is a great responsibility that requires wisdom, integrity, and patience. Being conscious of these dynamics, while also watching out for being self-centered, are the building blocks for handling power and authority correctly.

CHAPTER EIGHT

THE UNEXPECTED AND INEXPLICABLE

Life is the continuing intervention of the inexplicable.
—Erwin Chargaff

A young man took some drugs, then ended up at one of our local emergency rooms. Something happened at said ER and the young man wandered off, eventually finding his way onto the Texas Tech University campus. There he found a construction site, made his way down into a three-story deep hole, then climbed up a three-story high concrete form. Soon thereafter the Texas Tech University police were called and, after chatting with the young man, decided to call the Lubbock Police Department for assistance.

Two negotiators with LPD, Thomas and Jarred, arrived and quickly started a productive dialogue with the young man. As they chatted, numerous Lubbock Fire department vehicles and crews arrived, as well as other officers from our negotiating team. I got there fourth and was told the story I just told you. The young man was not excited about all the attention, and Thomas and Jarred relayed his demand that everyone stay out of sight nearby, behind a large mound of dirt.

Soon the young man was ready to come down, so Thomas and Jarred asked the fire department for a couple of their ladders. This request seemed to confuse or worry said firemen, as it took 30 minutes for them to obtain permission to give us two ladders and retrieve them from their truck parked about 40 feet away. During this unfortunate lag time, the substance our young man had ingested lost its potency and his high was gone. As is typical when coming off a drug bender, he then became quite sleepy. You can see from the two photos below that the young man did what any other sleepy person would do—he laid down on top of this concrete form to go night-night.

The young man wrapped himself in his recently-acquired hospital blanket and settled in. Deciding we no longer needed to hide behind the mound of dirt, we gathered together to confer about how best to proceed. Some in our gathering felt compelled by the "action imperative." This is a condition that often infects hard chargers, command staff, and elements of the public, and causes them to feel the pressure and anxiety to do something *right now*. My perspective was a bit different, and I shared it with those gathered. My man was asleep and relatively secure on his perch. Let's brainstorm and deliberately formulate a plan to put into action. Let's take our time and even entertain bad ideas.

A bad idea soon presented itself. How about we inject him with a sedative and then we can take him into custody. In an effort not to totally humiliate the one with this idea, we consulted a nearby EMS medic, who looked at us like we were purple, and then explained that the prick of the injection might wake my guy, and the sedative (if administered in the correct dosage so as not to kill my guy who'd just come off of some unknown substance) would probably take over a minute to take effect. The dumb idea was now properly contained and we moved on.

I asked the fire department battalion chief what he thought about using their spiffy bucket truck to reach out over our guy and pluck him to safety. The thoughtful battalion chief considered it, and I joked about this not being a scenario they'd previously trained on. He chuckled and then agreed that this might be our best approach. As we all continued to discuss how many police officers and how many firemen should be in the bucket, one of the firemen walked by the end of the metal ladders that had been placed across the hole and violently kicked/tripped over it.

We all shuddered and froze, our eyes fixed on our "jumper." The loud explosion of metal ladder noise caused him to raise his head sleepily; then he tucked himself deeper into the concrete form and pulled his blankee up to his chin. He returned to his slumber easily, and we all exhaled. I got on the radio and asked, "Could we not kick that ladder again, please?!" I later learned my plea made it onto the dispatch call sheet, which I promptly printed out for my scrapbook.

Our debate about how many firemen and how many negotiators would occupy the fire truck's bucket resumed, with the firemen losing out. If our guy decided he wasn't a morning person and wanted to fight, two officers would be better than one. With everyone now on the same page, our negotiators suited up in harnesses, climbing helmets, and the fire department got them ready to deploy. The large fire truck was put in place about 100 feet on the other side of the construction hole and everything was ready.

The other negotiators and I stayed in our place, right across the hole from our sleeping beauty. The two negotiators rode in the bucket across the hole, and it was a very slow ride for them. The fireman operating the bucket was clearly an expert, and had our guys placed perfectly next to/over our subject (see photo below).

It's difficult to make out our subject, but he is there, snuggled down in that concrete form with a fire department bucket hovering over him. The bright light in the distance is from the bucket truck, and helps give some perspective about how long of a ride across it was for the negotiators. The negotiators were in place and, as you can see from the photo, they opened the door on the bucket and prepared to invite our subject inside.

You can also see the ladders still in place, and the rest of us watched from the end of those ladders. Thomas opened the door, leaned down and called out the name of our subject. He told him it was time to get up and come with him, and pulled him into the bucket, as Jarred held on to Thomas. Our subject was quite grumpy upon being roused from his nest, and the fight was on. Thomas and Jarred tried to give him a big yank into the bucket, but unfortunately our subject's foot was caught down in the concrete form and was stuck. Those of us across the ditch could see this clearly, but Thomas and Jarred could not. They were very focused on not dropping our subject and getting him into the bucket quickly and efficiently, so they gave him another big yank. We all tried to tell them that his foot was stuck, but Thomas and Jarred could not hear us through the fighting and yelling from our subject. Luckily, on the next big yank our subject turned his leg correctly and everyone landed in a heap, safely inside the bucket.

The fight continued on once inside the bucket, and the bucket slowly made its way back across the construction hole. We all made our way around to the firetruck, ready to take over the fight from Thomas and Jarred. Well, I wasn't going to fight, since I'm just a civilian, but I did want a good vantage point.

We watched with anxiety as the bucket continued its long journey to us, and saw the flailing of mic cords and limbs as it did. Once to shore, everyone exited and our subject was in custody. Thomas and Jarred happily posed for a photo in their climbing helmets and harnesses, and everyone was safe. It was a good training day with the fire department, and it was nice to all work together, aside from the difficulties we had with the ladders.

*****

There was a 2-3 month period in which the negotiators at LPD responded to a number of people threatening to jump off of an overpass or parking garage. In this case, the parking garage was at a local hospital complex, and we were called to assist the patrol officers speaking with a young man sitting on the top floor of the garage with his legs over the edge of the guardrail (see below).

When I arrived, one of our negotiators was standing with the two patrol officers and acting as a coach, or secondary negotiator. Kimberlee was trying to assist them as well by taking up a position to relay information. She had a position around a cement wall and out of sight of the suicidal subject.

As you can see, she had a dry erase board and was trying to feed David (our negotiator in the light-colored suit shirt and tactical vest) information, questions to ask, and other helpful ideas. I stood behind Kimberlee and tried to assist her. We also wrote questions that David could answer for us with a yes or no (e.g. Are negotiations going well? Can we bring you some water? Do we need to get the ropes and harnesses in place?). We also asked questions that were more difficult for David to answer, so he would text us when he had a chance, and even sent us a photo of how things looked, since we could not see our subject. David sent us this photo about 20 minutes after I arrived (see below).

For me this photo represented progress, and our subject's position was much better than what we saw in the first photo. I like the distance we have between us and him, because it is possible that he might grab an officer as he fell and take the officer over the side with him, and I like that it is a calm conversation. We asked David how the officer speaking with him was doing, and David gave us a thumbs-up. We all settled in for what could be a long conversation, and continued to brainstorm about how to help David and the officer who was speaking to our subject.

This photo also represents the emotions of our subject. There are a number of possible emotions this man could be experiencing, and to consider them, and even talk about them with him, can be very helpful. It is easy to underestimate the value of putting words to emotions, and then saying those words to another person. In my work as a counselor, I often see the relief that comes to people when they simply say out loud what they have been thinking and feeling. Many people do not take the time to consider the emotions of another person, especially in a crisis, but this can be key to resolution. Sometimes people do not have the words, or are not ready to say them out loud. For the person listening to try and express these things and find the right words can also be helpful. For instance, when looking at the above photo one might see the emotion of desperation, or loneliness, or might just simply see pain. To offer one of these possibilities out loud can sometimes be helpful to the person in crisis (e.g. "As we talk, it looks to me like you are in pain. Is this correct?").

More of our team arrived, and some got our rope and harness system ready in case it was needed. In David's judgement, it was best to leave all that alone and continue on with what was working so far. There were a few times when David looked at us and frowned, indicating our subject was not doing well and might jump or fall. David knew what to tell the officer speaking to our subject, in order to try and disrupt our subject's train of thought that was leading him to jump (e.g. shouting out our subject's name or making statements about the realities associated with his decision to jump). These few precarious moments did not seem to last long, and David would indicate to us when he was doing better.

At some point one of the officers noticed a hospital bracelet on our subject's wrist, so some of the negotiators contacted the hospitals to try and identify the man with whom we were negotiating. We soon received our subject's name and passed it along via Kimberlee's dry erase board. We also learned that our subject had a long and difficult history of homelessness, relationship troubles, and drug abuse. He'd been to a local emergency room, but was asked to leave, and now he was here.

As this conversation unfolded over the next hour or so, the officers slowly moved closer to our subject, with his consent. It made it easier to hear him, and also helped with the human connection, when safe to do so. Kimberlee and I could not hear the conversation, so we were flying blind, other than the general tone of it all. I spoke with a few of our negotiators and our negotiating sergeant about the possibility of needing a quick reaction, should the situation change, or our subject decide to come down. We positioned a couple of negotiators whose job would be to rush around the corner and assist. One of these officers, Zach, was first in line and I was to give him the "go" signal if needed. After a few minutes, David indicated things were going well, and so I gave Zach a thumbs-up, just to keep him in the loop. His eyes got wide and he asked, Do we go?! My bad...Zach and I then worked out the "go signal" so we wouldn't have a malfunction. How tragic might it have been had Zach unnecessarily rushed around the corner to assist, all because I did not communicate clearly how we would initiate a response? It is wise to be clear, precise, and deliberate in a crisis.

There was a time a while ago when we were on the loudhailer outside of a suspect's house. There'd been no response and our negotiator asked the subject to give a sign that he was able to hear them. Then we heard a gunshot. Be specific regarding the type of sign you'd like!

After about an hour, David indicated that negotiations were stalled. It didn't seem our subject was going to kill himself, but he also was not willing to come down for us. David was able to text us a little, periodically, so I texted him that we were going to send him and the patrol officer speaking with him three bottles of water. I suggested that David and the patrol officer speaking with our subject drink the water like it was the best, most refreshing water they'd ever had. Eventually, David read my text, smirked, and nodded. We sent over a few bottles of water and the patrol officer offered one to our subject, who refused it. David and the patrol officer drank greedily, and thoroughly enjoyed it.

I then reached into my beloved vest and pulled out a couple of granola bars that had been in there for years. The summer heat in my car had made them rock solid, but I decided to send them over anyway. I knew David would bite into it and give me a "what the?" look. Morale and perspective in these situations are important, so I went with it. David knew intuitively that he and the patrol officer would need to eat these bars in similar fashion as they drank the water, so I sat back to enjoy their improvisation and acting skills. The purpose here was to keep things light and flexible since negotiating can be a tedious emotional rollercoaster. It may not be wise to spring jokes on your teammates in the middle of a tense and life-threatening negotiation; however, when you know your teammates well and you know you will improve the situation at hand, a light-hearted touch can go a long way.

I watched David try to take a bite, and then smirk. He happily handed one to the patrol officer, because David is as evil as I am. They both "enjoyed" their snack, and about five minutes later our subject came down to enjoy a little food of his own. When he came down, I gave Zach our pre-agreed upon signal, and everyone gently but efficiently gathered around our subject. The patrol officer did a great job of speaking with our subject, and was respectful and caring as he continued his conversation with him. The patrol officer was also very grateful for our team's assistance and support, and we all thoroughly enjoyed working together as a team.

*****

Another one of these calls to assist someone threatening to jump was at a different parking garage, yet at the same hospital complex in town. This time, we were not on the top floor, but were still three or four stories high. Our female subject was lying on her stomach on the cement guardrail, one arm and leg on our side, the others outside. She was also on the phone. Slowly and calmly, as though nothing scary was going on, I made my way towards the woman on the ledge, and joined the four LPD negotiators already speaking with her. Zach was the primary negotiator on this one, and he is very good at thinking on his feet and responding naturally and quickly to anything thrown at him. He was working hard, yet was calm and caring.

If memory serves, we were up there with her for a couple hours. In my 20 years of doing this, the most afraid I have ever been about someone jumping or falling was in the first story I shared in chapter one, and in this current callout. I was scared in the first story because the man's heels were over the edge and we had no idea what was going on with him. His heightened emotional state and unpredictability, along with his precarious perch, were quite frightening. In this current situation, there were a number of times when it seemed plain to all of us that this woman was going to slip over the side of that ledge and fall four stories to the concrete below. During those times in which it seemed imminent that she was going to let herself fall, I passed a three-by-five notecard to Zach with things on it I've never suggested before. It seemed clear to all of us we had to do all we could to stop her, and it was time to use every tool in our toolkit.

I had the honor this past summer to be invited to Scotland to observe how the United Kingdom trains their negotiators. If you want to become a negotiator in the UK, you must apply to this course, or its sister course in London, and it is pass/fail. It lasts for two weeks, and you must pass week one before you can attend the second week of the course. Each day of training begins at 8:30 am and goes until about 10:00 pm. The day is a combination of lecture, exercises, scenarios, feedback, and practice, and it is a thorough way of getting negotiators prepared for the real thing. At the end of the second week, you learn whether or not you can become a negotiator.

Early in the course, students were presented with a picture on the screen of a man threatening to jump from a bridge. Each student in turn was called to the front of the room to negotiate with the man, and over time the picture would change. It changed from him near the edge, to climbing over the edge of the barrier, to being on the ledge, to looking like he was about to jump. As the man grew closer and closer to jumping, it was interesting to watch these untrained negotiators do their best to talk to the unresponsive screen. When it looked like the man was about to jump, the negotiating student continued on his dialogue without any urgency, just as the students before him had done. It was at this point one of the instructors, Frasier, jumped in to show them how it's done. Frasier yelled, and pleaded, and warned, and threw everything he could think of at this man in order to break him out of his current line of thinking, and possibly shock him back into coherence. This moment for our team, there with this woman in the parking garage, was the real-life equivalent.

I quickly but clearly wrote on my three-by-five note card everything I could think of to shock this woman into not slipping away from us and into outer space. I handed it to Zach's coach, who gave it to him. He was tracking with me and quickly said some of the lines I wrote, but in his words and in the context of his conversation and relationship with this woman. He said her name, then said things like, "The fall may not kill you. You may end up broken and in the hospital, unable to care for your husband and children", and other reality checks.

When hit with these thoughts, these doubts, these things to consider, she shifted her hips back towards us, and Zach thanked her. It costs us nothing to be courteous, and we exhaled internally. Our subject neared this line a couple more times over the course of the next hour, and I handed Zach more three-by-five cards, and he did everything he could to try to stop her from slipping away from us.

At other times during this conversation she was on the phone with her therapist. We tried to figure out who the therapist was so we could send a negotiator to her to help her, support her, and even coach her. As best we could tell, this woman's conversation with her therapist was also helpful, although we worried about conflicting purposes. It is so often a difficult thing to contain our conversations with people. From the crowds down below shouting unhelpful encouragements, to people posting on Facebook or calling their family, it is very difficult to have a focused conversation with someone in crisis or holding hostages.

As I usually do, I went back and forth between our group of negotiators and the negotiators and command staff gathered about 20 yards away, and gave them an update and assessment of how things were going. They sometimes had feedback or things for us to consider, so I passed this along to our group of negotiators. Our rope system and harness were on-scene, and we all prepared to set it up and get Zach in a harness.

As our team got things set up and laid out, our subject did not like what was going on. She made it known quickly and everyone stopped what they were doing. She was afraid and she started to shift her hips away from us again. Zach did a great job of reassuring her and we abandoned getting our ropes and harnesses in place.

After a few hours, our subject agreed to Zach's caring but firm statements that it was time to come down now. However, because of her straddled position on that guardrail, she was stuck with one leg on each side. Zach offered to come help her, but she refused, stating she was scared. We asked her to put her phone down, which she eventually did, but she still could not get her outside leg back to the inside. Our offers to help her down were refused, and it seemed we were stuck.

Earlier we had tied a rope off to a police Tahoe and the sight of us putting on harnesses scared her. Now Zach offered her that rope and, surprisingly, she agreed to take it. I handed the rope to Zach, and he calmly and with reassurance slowly walked up to her and handed her the rope. He let her struggle to reach out and eventually grab the rope, then asked if he could help her over. The combination of grabbing the rope, and then the rest of us helping her over, did the trick and she was safe. We handed her the rope… what a perfect metaphor for what we do.

We surrounded her and reassured her as she lay on the ground and recovered. We told her she made the right decision, even though she did not want to. We thanked her and told her we were proud of her.

Zach accompanied her to the ER, and I caught up with them shortly. We met with her husband to let him know all that had happened. Her demeanor changed a bit as she talked with the ER staff, and it seemed she was downplaying the crisis she was in earlier. We gave her our best for those few hours, and now it was time to hand off her care to others, hoping she would get the help she needed and accept the help being offered.

Later that afternoon I called her therapist, the one who'd been on the phone with her while she was on that concrete guardrail. It seemed to me the therapist might need to debrief, and it seemed the right thing to do to let her know what happened after they hung up. The therapist could hear in our voices our concern when it looked like our subject was about to fall. The therapist could not see what was going on, but could tell it was bad at those points in the conversation. It was helpful for her to talk through this with me, and get more information about what we were thinking and trying to accomplish. I thanked her for her help, and for not working against us. She said that she kept encouraging her counseling client to trust us and that we were there to help. It was so nice to have her working with us; all of us working together in the same ways towards the same goals.

A couple of months later, I was boarding a plane to go speak at a negotiator conference. I hate missing callouts, and had so far not missed a thing because I was out of town. As I sat in the terminal at the Lubbock International Airport, our text notification system went off: Negotiator Only Callout, jumper, Marsha Sharp Freeway. I texted the group to let them know I'd be on a plane soon, but was able to help out by phone as needed.

Our negotiators arrived at the freeway overpass and texted updates to the rest of the team. The woman on the ledge was on her phone while also talking to an officer who used to be on our negotiating team. Others from our team arrived to assist, and eventually the text came across letting everyone know that this was the woman from the hospital parking garage a couple of months earlier. I'd never assisted with the same suicidal jumper twice.

Soon Zach arrived on-scene, and the negotiators there made the transition. I texted a few reminders to everyone about how best to negotiate with this woman (caring, but firm, almost parental, but not authoritarian), and stood by to see if there was anything else I could do to help. Someone asked about contacting her therapist again, and I offered to do so. At this point, the boarding announcement came across the PA in the airport and I started to feel pressed for time. I called the therapist, who let me know she'd moved away. She gave me the name of the woman's current therapist, who I knew, and I gave her a call.

The therapist was on the phone with her as she was on the outside of the guardrail (see below).

Though it looks like our subject was listening to her iPod, she was actually talking on her cell phone with the therapist. I asked the therapist where she was, and then texted the negotiators on scene, asking if one of them could go and coach/assist the therapist. Kimberlee answered up and was enroute. Here's a view of the little outcropping our subject was trying to stand on, while on the phone with her therapist, and beginning her dialogue with Zach.

Zach picked up the conversation with her and asked her how things had been going since they last spoke. He remembered the right tone and stance to take with her, and didn't get too emotional when she tried to test him. He knew which subjects to avoid, and what to emphasize. Pretty quickly she was ready to come down, and Zach had to figure out how to help her without 1) her accidently falling, and 2) him being pulled over with her.

She began to make her way around the light pole, and briefly lost her footing. Zach slowed her down, talked her through the step-by-step process of how to safely get over the railing, and let her know what he was going to do. Zach knew he needed to keep a low center of gravity, and waiting for the ropes system to arrive was not an option, especially considering how she reacted to them the last time. He knelt so his center of gravity was low. The negotiators with him also were right there ready to grab him and/or help her come over the guardrail. Meanwhile, I boarded my plane.

I was intent on my phone as I put up my bag and got seated. It was a bit surreal to be sitting on a plane, watching the people around me do as everyone usually does when getting settled on a plane, yet the drama playing out on the other side of my phone was not something anyone could really understand. Nor could I explain it to them sufficiently. The woman next to me noticed my demeanor, and asked me about it. I gave her a quick overview, but was brief and light on details because she was a stranger and I had no idea how she'd react to my job, much less to what I've been doing via text the last 30 minutes. But she was understanding and encouraging, and I let her know how things resolved after our plane landed. I was so glad it was only a 50-minute flight from Lubbock to Dallas, especially since I couldn't receive texts while on that flight.

So, as the flight attendants were singing their familiar song and doing the familiar dance in the aisles, here's a picture of what Zach was doing (see below).

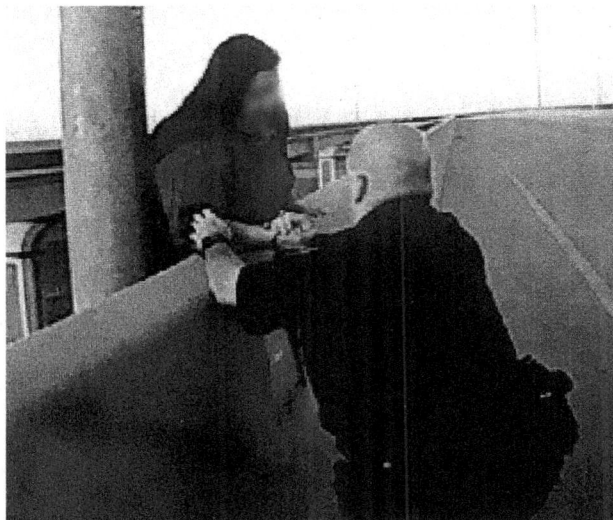

Zach helped her over the side once again, and she was safe. It's so hard to explain to people what this work is like, especially when sitting next to them on a plane. It's hard to explain how personal this work is. It's hard to express the cost of empathy and the investment of time, training, and our work on-scene when training turns into real-life. This photo captures a bit of that for me. Zach kneeling, caring for, giving his all for someone in crisis, after spending so much time trying to help, bringing to bear all his training and all he knows about her, while also trying to be flexible, mentally agile, open, and—most important—listen.

CHAPTER NINE

RESPONDING TO THE HORRIFIC

[1]But mark this: There will be terrible times in the last days. [2]People will be lovers of themselves, lovers of money, boastful, proud, abusive, disobedient to their parents, ungrateful, unholy, [3]without love, unforgiving, slanderous, without self-control, brutal, not lovers of the good, [4]treacherous, rash, conceited, lovers of pleasure rather than lovers of God— [5]having a form of godliness but denying its power. —2 Timothy 3:1-5

Perspective. It's amazing how life works out. There's all these crazy stories and amazing outcomes, and then there's the overall view as well. In 2014, I got my dissertation published in the *Journal of Emergency Mental Health*. When I received my issue, I also looked at the other articles published, and the one just below mine caught my attention. I would later become friends with the author, Amy, who later made a trip from England to Lubbock to do some research and interviews with me and our negotiators. I saw in Amy's article her recommendations for doing research with hostage (crisis) negotiators. It sounded simple enough, and I knew some negotiators, so I gave it a go. A few years later, I had my research on negotiators published and shared it with the negotiators who participated, one of whom was the team leader for the negotiating team in my hometown of Bellevue, Washington. That team leader just so happened to be on the board for the Western States Hostage Negotiator Association (WSHNA), and WSHNA just so happened to be holding their upcoming yearly conference in Bellevue. Because I had shared my results with this team leader, he invited me to speak at the conference and share the results (see the references at the end of this book for that citation if you would like to read more). The next thing I knew, I was in my hometown at the conference that just so happened to be held in a local hotel my high school friends and I used to run around in! This speaking opportunity led to others, and now I am speaking internationally on the topics of crisis intervention and crisis negotiating. At the conference, I also met Kevin Briggs, who wrote the foreword for my first book of stories. You never know how life will lead you, and lead you back over familiar ground. It's almost impossible to have perspective without the benefit of hindsight and taking the time to review.

In my first book, I shared a number of heart-breaking stories, and since then I have been involved with some more. A recent example was a Critical Incident Stress Management debriefing I helped lead for some deputies and fire fighters who responded to a fire in a mobile home. The mother of four children left for work, and left her children sleeping under the care of her new boyfriend, who subsequently decided to leave the residence to meet another woman. While he was gone, a space heater caught the home on fire and all four children died. I learned about all the details of responding to this scene from the deputies and fire fighters who were at the debriefing, and they were all devastated by the senseless loss of innocent life, and this because of someone's selfish desires. But for them, this tragedy was overshadowed by one event in particular. One of the little girls was pulled from the home and, after life-saving efforts proved useless, was covered in a blanket in the front yard. The deputies wept as they recounted how the firefighters finished their work on the structure, then gathered around this little girl to kneel and pray.

It is extremely difficult to continue to face and respond to the darkness at work in the lives of people. It can take a terrible toll to be that close to selfishness, darkness, and evil, and sometimes it can change a person. If you maintain yourself, and a proper perspective, then you can thrive in this field. The parable of the man saving a viper from a fire has been helpful in this regard. A man once pulled a viper from a fire, only to be bitten by the viper even as he tried to save it. The man maintained his composure and rested the viper nearby. As it scurried off, the man's friend, incredulous, asked why he hadn't flung the viper back into the fire for attacking him. The man responded, "The viper did what vipers do. This does not change who I am or why I set about to rescue it in the first place." Dr. Martin Luther King Jr. famously said, "Darkness cannot drive out darkness; only light can do that. Hate cannot drive out hate; only love can do that."

To maintain oneself even in the worst of situations is the true test of one's character. If your character changes due to circumstances, then it was not your character in the first place. We cannot endeavor to address the darkness and pain in others if we do not first have our own identity in place and firmly established. We must be able to embody love if we have any hope of addressing the lack of it in others. We cannot truly heal others if we do not embody the healing power of love. To ruminate about the dark will not change it. We can consider how we could have responded better, but then we must continue to be who we are and be about the business of giving the world an alternative to the behaviors that come naturally to those who are self-centered. These are the truths that will help us have the perspective of a Dr. Martin Luther King Jr., or the man who was attacked by a viper as he tried to save it.

Perspective is everything when it comes to responding to the situations law enforcement is often called into. People are often ruled by fear, and may respond out of fear in ways that look threatening. An example I heard recently was of a traffic stop in which the driver was pulled over and refused to roll down his window or obey commands to exit his vehicle. The driver sat in his seat like a statue with his hands on the wheel. SWAT and negotiators responded, and many responding officers viewed this driver's noncompliance as a threat. Even so, officers carefully approached the driver again and tried to communicate. The driver turned his head and looked at the officers, but did not move or otherwise respond. After a while, the negotiator wrote on a piece of paper, "Please exit your car. We would like to speak with you." The driver responded with sign language.

The perspective we have during a crisis, and about its origins and causes, influences and even governs our responses. Keeping an open mind, and looking for all the possibilities and motivations behind someone's behavior can keep law enforcement from making critical errors. A team approach can help with this endeavor, especially when that team has a lot of training and experience together. A team that is cohesive and cares for each other can also help mitigate the effects of working in these dark and disturbing environments.

About midway through my presentation I did recently, I shared my perspective on how to maintain oneself when trying to help others, even when they do atrocious things, aren't buying the help we are selling, or are just outright hell-bent on their own destruction. I then got a question from a counselor who was just in pieces after trying to help a suicidal teenager. This counselor had given of herself, and had put her time, heart, and soul into helping this teen stay alive, and even heal. It was painfully apparent to the 200 mental health professionals in the room that this woman embodied the care and passion we all had to some degree, and she was dying for answers. I outlined for her the limitations of our power and authority to help people, even those who are on a path to their own death. I recounted how we cannot allow this to make us become jaded or hopeless, and that we do the best with what we have. Somewhere, early in my answer, her crying overcame her and she had to leave the room. The audience was shaken and moved, and then all looked at me. I continued to answer her as if she was still present, and the audience seemed to agree with my philosophy of helping. We have to accept our limitations, while at the same time, give the best we know at that time. I then turned to the audience and professed that, were it my loved one who wanted to die, I would want the audience to also have the care, compassion, empathy, and tenacity that I saw in the woman who was now down the hall crying in the bathroom.

I continued my speech, and wrapped up about the time the woman returned to my session. As people came to the front of the room to chat, I made a beeline to her as she made a beeline to me. She apologized for her outburst of emotion, but I stopped her. I told her what I said to the audience about how I would want her to be the one to help any loved one of mine who was in the throes of crisis. She was sweet, and relieved to have been able to tell her story, share her frustration, and cry out her empathy. She was very happy for the support, and I thanked her for her bravery in asking this all-too-important question. The darkness was starting to overcome her, and if it did, there would be less help available to the people in her sphere of influence. She was needed, and she needed to let down, heal, and get ready to go back out there. We all benefitted from her question, and this overall discussion. We cannot do this alone, and we cannot carry on without the proper perspective. Love doesn't win every battle, but it will win the war.

AFTERWORD

In my first book, I opened by sharing a very difficult start to my work with law enforcement. This included a time in July 2001 when our department suffered two separate deaths of officers in the line of duty over the course of less than a week. One of those deaths was the tragic loss of Sgt. Kevin Cox. Trying to assist grieving officers and their families, attending the funerals, navigating political fallout, and the million other little things that go along with these events was very difficult, especially because I had never done this work before, and because we had to call outside agencies (strangers) for assistance.

Nineteen years later, right after I finished writing this book, tragedy struck again. One of our officers and two firefighters were struck by a car while working a traffic wreck on an icy highway. One of the firefighters, and our officer, Nicholas Reyna, died, and once again it was time to assist our department in navigating and coping with a devastating loss. I got a call about the fatality, and was asked to assist Lt. John Hayes with the death notification. John and I went to college together, and he started with LPD about a year before I did. We met, and walked upstairs to the officer's apartment and knocked on the door to deliver the news to his 27-year-old wife and one-year-old daughter. What happened on the other side of that door is hallowed ground, and is still too fresh to recount.

For the next week, John and I did all we could for Nick's family, including trying to help them come to terms with this new and horrible reality. We will forever be bound to this new widow, and John put it best when he said that this was the most amazing and horrible experience of his life. We walked with the widow through the funeral and related events. We followed her husband's casket through the path lined by honor guard members from all around, standing at attention and saluting. We wept as the dispatcher on the radio called and called for Nick, but was only met with silence. We stood with her, knelt with her, handed her tissues, and prayed with her. We walked that hallowed ground and were forever changed.

At the graveside service, she was presented with a flag, just as you see in the movies at the funeral of a United States service member. We sat next to her and listened to the words of comfort offered by dignitaries, strangers, friends, and loved ones. We listened to heavy sobs, to Amazing Grace played on the bagpipes, to a state police helicopter flyover, to the deafening silence of the gathered crowd, to the shocking sound of a 21-gun salute, to a rider-less horse clip clopping by, and to Taps.

At the beginning of the funeral, she wanted time alone with Nick, but asked me to stand beside her. At the end of the graveside service she wanted to be away from the crowd and with her husband as he was lowered into the ground. John and I stood beside her. The LPD honor guard was with her too. Here are a couple photos of the honor guard gathered around her, and depict a sweet and deeply touching moment from that day.

John and I are so glad she got to have this time with the honor guard; the officers who stood with Nick from the time he was killed until he was laid to rest. We hope it was healing for her, and I know this time with her was healing for them. They saluted his casket as it was lowered into the ground. They would have done so had we not been there. She got to throw the first handful of dirt into the grave, and she got to take her time. They folded again the American flag that draped her husband's casket because it became a little loose as we left the larger ceremony. They did so with the same formality and respect as during the larger ceremony with dignitaries. This time, the sergeant in charge of the honor guard took possession of the flag, marched over to Lt. John Hayes, who had been with her since we knocked on her door with that horrible news, and gave it to him. According to protocol, the highest-ranking officer presents the flag to the family member. John then had the honor of presenting the flag to her for the final time, and I got to choke back tears.

I am not sure people realize the cost of empathy and love. I could see it in the honor guard, who cared deeply for Nick and his family. They took seriously their role in standing guard over Nick, and in making known how much Nick mattered. His death affected everyone, the honor guard included, as it should, because Nick was a good man doing a good work.

I took a few moments to walk to a nearby grave, that of Sgt. Kevin Cox. I remembered all that LPD had been through, all I experienced in 2001, and even experienced some of the emotions that I did not have time for back then. I had more time to grieve and experience everything this time around because of all the help around me from people I knew and trusted. From our Critical Incident Stress Management teams who took care of officers while I assisted the family, to our Victim Services Crisis team who went to the scene of the accident, to the hospital, and to the police department to assist the grieving, and all of the support I received personally from all of my friends at LPD. It was so good to walk through this valley of the shadow of death, but to not do so alone. My beloved vest, which can protect from all sorts of weaponry, cannot protect me from my emotions. Something else was required.

Bookends. My first book began with, and this book concludes with, the death of a police officer. It has been an amazing 20 years, and some of the most emotional and powerful work anyone could do. I stand amazed at the privilege it has been to walk these hallowed grounds with such amazing people, and outline how to care well for people. From embodying the virtues, such as patience, empathy, kindness, integrity, and selflessness, to maintaining the proper perspective while in a crisis, to levity. These are the virtues that can help heal others and make us better people, all at the same time.

REFERENCES, RECOMMENDATIONS AND RESOURCES

For assistance with the grief associated with the death of a child: www.compassionatefriends.org

Barrick, M., and Mount, M., "Yes Personality Matters: Moving on to More Important Matters." *Human Performance, 18* (4), 2005, 359-372.

Frankl, V., *Man's Search for Meaning.* (Boston: Beacon Press, 1959).

Gilliland, James R., and Gilliland, B., (2013). *Crisis Intervention Strategies.* (Boston: Brooks/Cole Publishing, 2013).

Gilmartin, K., *Emotional Survival for Law Enforcement: A Guide for Officers and Their Families.* (Tucson: E-S Press, 2002).

Jamison, K., *Night Falls Fast: Understanding Suicide.* (New York: Knopf Doubleday Publishing Group, 2000).

Kirshman, E. *I Love a Cop.* (New York: Guilford Press, 2006).

Lord J., and Stewart A., *I'll Never Forget Those Words: A Practical Guide to Death Notification.* (Burnsville: Compassion Press, 2008).

Mitchell, J., and Everly, G., *Critical Incident Stress Debriefing: An Operations Manual for CISD, Defusing and Other Group Crisis Intervention Services.* (Columbia: Chevron Publishing, 2001).

Pinizzotto, A., Kern, H., and Davis, E., "One-Shot Drops: Surviving the Myth." *FBI Law Enforcement Bulletin.* (Washington: Federal Bureau of Investigation, U.S. Department of Justice, October, 2004).

Yalom, I., and Leszcz, M., *The Theory and Practice of Group Psychotherapy, Fifth Edition.* (New York, Basic Books, 2005).

Young, A., Fuller, J., and Riley, B., "On-scene Mental Health Counseling Provided through Police Departments." *Journal of Mental Health Counseling, Volume 30, Number 4*, 345-361.

Young, A., and Brumley, N., "On-scene Mental Health Services: A Case Study of the Lubbock Police Department's Victims Services Crisis Team." *FBI Law Enforcement Bulletin. 6-11.* (Washington: Federal Bureau of Investigation, U.S. Department of Justice, September, 2009).

Young, A., Hennington, C., and Eggleston, D. "US SWAT Operator Experience, Personality, Cognitive-Emotion Regulation and Decision-Making Style." *Policing: An International Journal, 41* (2), 2018, 247-261.

Young, A., "Police Hostage (Crisis) Negotiators in the US: A National Survey". *Journal of Police and Criminal Psychology, 31 (4)*, 2016, 310-321.

Young, A., *Fight or Flight: Negotiating Crisis on the Frontline.* (Chambersburg: eGen Publishing, 2015).

GLOSSARY

Bad guy – Someone who obviously committed a crime and is probably the focus of the attention of law enforcement.

Command post – In the case of a SWAT callout, the area in which commanders and chiefs have gathered to command and control the crisis response. Often the command post begins as command staff gathered in the street together, and then moves to a mobile command post like a departmental RV that is outfitted for such an event.

Counseling/counselor – In the state of Texas it is someone who has obtained a graduate degree in counseling or a related field, taken the state licensing exam, completed 3000 hours of supervised counseling, and now operates according to the standards of practice outlined by the state board of ethics.

Crisis – An event that overwhelms an individual's ability to cope.

Crisis intervention or Psychological First Aid – Methods and strategies for assisting people in crisis and the situations surrounding a crisis.

Critical Incident Stress Management (CISM) – A model and protocols by Mitchell and Everly designed to assist emergency services personnel with psychologically processing stressful or traumatic events.

Diagnostic and Statistical Manual of Mental Disorders V – The current edition of the manual that contains the diagnostic criteria for psychological and mental disorders.

Domestic violence – Violence perpetrated by a family member upon another family member.

Emergency medical services (EMS) – A service that provides emergency medical care outside of the hospital. Emergency medical technicians and paramedics typically provide this care.

Gallows humor – A type of humor that is found in dark and depressing situations, usually used as a coping mechanism. I have many examples, but I fear they all could be offensive, especially without proper attitude and context.

Good guy – Everyone who is not a bad guy.

Homicide – When a person's death is caused by the actions of another person.

Hostage – Someone held by force against their will and who often is used as leverage in negotiations.

Hostage or Crisis Negotiator – A specially-trained law enforcement officer who often responds to SWAT callouts and other situations where dialogue with someone may assist in the peaceful resolution of an incident.

> **Primary negotiator** – A negotiator who speaks directly to a subject.

> **Secondary negotiator** – A negotiator who assists the primary negotiator and serves as the funnel through which all communication with the primary negotiator passes.

Medical examiner – A physician licensed by the state to investigate the medical causes of death.

Mental health professional – A general term from someone educated and usually licensed by the state as a counselor, social worker, therapist, psychologist, psychiatrist, etc.

Police titles:

    Cadet – A person training to be a police officer through a police academy.

    Captain – A police officer of high rank, above that of lieutenant, that typically is responsible for command decisions.

    Chief of police – The most senior police officer in charge of all police within a city or jurisdiction.

    Commissioner – A police officer in charge of a particular police force.

    Cop – A term for a police officer that is usually not derogative.

    Corporal – A rank above that of police officer.

    Deputy – A law enforcement officer in a County Sheriff's Department.

    Detective – A police officer who investigates criminal activity and presents findings to a district attorney.

    Lieutenant – A rank above that of sergeant and usually denotes command responsibilities.

    Patrolman - A police officer of entry rank assigned to the patrol division of a department.

    Sergeant – A police officer of middle rank, below that of lieutenant, usually responsible for the supervision of officers and corporals.

Sheriff – The most senior law enforcement officer in a county.

State trooper – A police officer who is a member of a state police force.

Post-traumatic stress disorder (PTSD) – A psychological disorder that is caused by exposure to a traumatic event and includes specific symptoms from a list of categories such as avoidance (e.g. avoiding things associated with the traumatic event), intrusion (e.g. nightmares), and hypervigilance (e.g. being jumpy or on guard).

Psychological Consultant – A mental health professional attached to a crisis (hostage) negotiating team whose job description often includes providing feedback and input about negotiating strategies, assessment of the subject(s) involved, suicide and violence risk assessment, assisting with training, consultation, and sometimes acting as the primary negotiator, coach, or filling in other negotiating team roles.

Subject – The negotiating team is focused on this person, who could be in crisis, acting criminally, and/or is threatening to themselves or others.

Suicide by cop – Putting a law enforcement officer in the position of having to use deadly force for the purpose of causing one's own death.

SWAT (Special Weapons and Tactics) callout – A law enforcement incident determined to require a specialized response by officers specially trained and outfitted with the proper equipment. SWAT callouts typically involve responding to heavily armed subjects, barricaded subjects, hostage situations, and other incidents not easily or safely handled by patrol officers.

Third-party intermediary (TPI) – Using someone as a "go-between" during the process of negotiations.

Victim Services Crisis Team (VSCT) – A group of mental health professionals whose response is initiated by law enforcement in order to assist officers and/or civilians with a crisis situation.

ABOUT THE AUTHOR

Andy Young received a bachelor's degree in Bible from Lubbock Christian University in 1993, a master's degree in Youth and Family Ministry from Abilene Christian University in 1995, a master's in Community Counseling from Texas Tech University in 1999, and a doctorate in Counselor Education from Texas Tech University in 2003. He has been a professor at Lubbock Christian University since 1996 and currently teaches in the undergraduate Psychology and Counseling Department. He has also taught in the graduate Counseling, graduate Nursing, and undergraduate Bible Departments.

He has been working with the Lubbock Police Department since 2000 and the Lubbock County Sheriff's Office since 2008. Andy also currently serves on the negotiating teams for both agencies, and has recently joined the negotiating team at the Texas Department of Public Safety, Region 5. Additionally, he acts as clinical director for the Critical Incident Stress Management Teams for the South Plains Regional Response Team, the Lubbock Police Department, and the Lubbock Fire Department.

Young is also a founding member and current coordinator for the Lubbock Police Department's Victim Services Crisis Team, which has grown to about 40 members. He is the author of several published academic articles and speaks frequently on crisis intervention and hostage negotiation, most recently at hostage negotiator conferences sponsored by various state associations, including New York, California, Washington, and Texas.

Andy and his wife, Stacy, whom he married in 1995, live in Lubbock, Texas with their two children.

www.ingramcontent.com/pod-product-compliance
Lightning Source LLC
Chambersburg PA
CBHW050654270326
41927CB00012B/3028